DeAR Kelly c m̶̶̶̶̶̶̶̶̶ '9

Ps 119:27, Open up my understanding
to the ways of wisdom and I will
meditate deeply on your splendor
and your wonders!

May god richly bless you as you
serve HIM in all you do,
think c. are in Christ!
                Jesus loves you and so
            Do I.
                Linda
                    Kuehler

1

HEAVENLY HAPPENINGS

HOW THE GOD

OF HEAVEN

REVEALED HIMSELF TO ME

Authored By Linda Kuebler

COPYRIGHT 2018

PUBLISHED NOVEMBER 2018

ISBN: 9781790355228

CONTRIBUTIONS FROM BOB KUEBLER

PUBLISHED BY HEART STORM PUBLISHING

Cover Photo

The Cover Photo was taken by our great friend Jim Taylor. In this picture, Linda is thinking about the majesty of God's creation from her vantage point on top of Piano Pass. She's sitting on the edge of a precipice in the Grand Canyon overlooking Phantom Creek.

Thank you Jim Taylor for being such a good friend. Jesus loves you and so do we.

HEAVENLY HAPPENINGS

HOW THE GOD

OF HEAVEN

REVEALED HIMSELF TO ME

Author

Linda Kuebler

DEDICATION

This book is dedicated to my Spiritual Mother and forever friend Donna May. Donna opened my eyes to the reality of a God I never knew and loves me completely. From my heart I want to say thank you Donna for being a friend in the many seasons of my life. You've been my friend in times of laughter and in times of sadness. You've been my teacher and you believed in me. It's such a joy to know that we will share eternity together.

To my husband Bob, who is my constant companion and encourager. You are ever faithful and the only man who ever called me "Sveltey!" Without your love, guidance, skills and creative mind this book would never have happened. I love you my forever love.

"Heavenly Happenings takes you on a journey with Linda as she discovers how much God loves her and wants to have a relationship. She shares openly and honestly about her experiences as she chooses to grow in her relationship with the Lord. She shares practical examples that will encourage you in your walk with the Lord, which will make you want to pray and trust God for all things in your life. It was a privilege to get to listen in on her journey."

Patty Berens
Chaplain
Inspirational Speaker

"If you've ever wondered what an intimate, personal relationship with God looks like, Heavenly Happenings gives an inside look behind the scenes of life with Him. The author gives a candid narration of instances we would take for granted and shows us how she brought Jesus into those places. Her stories will spark a desire to grow closer to God whether you have known Him for years or are just now stepping into a relationship with Him. I have known the author personally for a long time and have had the privilege of watching her live out her faith with both boldness and intimacy. It is with great pleasure that I recommend you read Heavenly Happenings by Linda Kuebler."

Sally Smale,
Establishing Word Ministries

"What a delightful book to read. I loved the cover with Linda's picture and the bright colors. The title was perfect. I used the book like you would a devotional and read the stories one at a time, which took discipline. Each story had a moral and then verses at the end to uplift the reader. Of course, the best part of the book is how each story was a real experience in Linda's life. God seems to speak in a way that shows He is always present and interested in the details of each person's life."

Donna May
Author

"Through guidance from the Holy Spirit, Linda Kuebler explains the tangible presence of God in her life. Heavenly Happenings is an exceptional learning experience in trusting the Lord and being surrendered to Him for a life plan.

'Heavenly Happenings' includes frequent accounts of unexplainable miracles during Linda's daily walk with the Lord. Miracles that are not coincidental but orchestrated by Jesus to bless and teach her as she draws closer to Him through a growing faith and greater joy.

Linda describes hearing the Lord's voice in various ways from prayer to reading His Word while learning to obey God's leading and direction. She discerns the difference between being an individual who embraces Jesus in all her life choices from a church-going religious person who follows a set of rules."

Pamela Williams
Buffalo, New York

"Heavenly Happenings" draws readers into sensational accounts on a supernatural journey where Linda Kuebler has experienced a lifestyle of an intimate awareness of God. She shares how the abiding presence of the Lord Jesus is much more than living content with a blessed assurance that Heaven is an eternal abode; but, also how she came to anticipate and experience His Holy Spirit in heavenly places while on earth."

Dr. Pamala Denise Smith
GateView Ministries
Arizona

When I met this author many years ago, I had been a Christian several years...long years. I had read in Isaiah 9:6 that Jesus was born to us to be a "Wonderful Counselor," an "Everlasting Father," a "Prince of Peace"; but I certainly did not know Him as any of those things in my life. I was like the Ethiopian eunuch to whom Philip was sent in Acts 8:30. When Linda Kuebler befriended me, she began to invite me into stories and examples of how the Lord is speaking all the time, if we can only take that step of faith WITH Him to learn to hear, see, AND read in His Word with new eyes. Much the same way she does in this book!

Little by little, the reality she spoke of, became mine as well –the reality of God's profound unchanging love and the INTIMACY with Jesus, available to every one of us.

This is such a BEAUTIFUL BOOK. It is written in such a warm and personal way, the way a good friend shares stories of their life. As you read, you are not even aware that you are being immersed into a "mini instruction manual." You are enveloped into a series of stories about the way our loving Savior wants to walk with us, so that we, too, can "live, move and have our very being in Him" (Acts 17:28). Read on. Let the eyes of your heart be opened, and be Very Blessed!

Maria Caballero
Arizona

CONTENTS

INTRODUCTION

God is no "respecter of persons." My life journey began on a path of self-determination as I was totally focused on building a successful life according to the world's standards. Even though I ignored God, He never ignored me.

This book represents the desire of my heart to encourage people to open their eyes to the reality that God loves them completely. God reconciled the world to Himself in the person of Jesus Christ. I know how to love others because He first loved me the way I was. He saw me for what I could be in Him not for what I was in myself.

This collection of true stories represents what God has done in my life. I pray that reading them will encourage you to trust God with your whole heart, soul, mind and strength. To really live is to be totally surrendered to Him. He turns our weaknesses into strengths to be used for His glory in helping other people fully know His love.

Love is who God is. Love is what God wants to do through me and you. Love is what this book is about.

"The one who does not love
has not become acquainted with God
[does not and never did know Him],
for God is love.
[He is the originator of love,
and it is an enduring attribute of His nature.]"
1 John 4:8 Amplified Bible

CHAPTER ONE

I FOUND WHAT WAS MISSING!

Most people looking at my life would view me as a very successful business person. At 31 years old, I was a co-partner in the ownership of a hair salon. We made fairly good money which gave me lots of worldly pleasures like a fancy car and a townhouse. I also had a shallow relationship with an uncommitted boyfriend. Well, at least most of my life looked successful! As successful as I was, I knew that something was missing. My success didn't bring me much in the way of happiness. There was a deep and empty hollowness in my heart.

Our lunch room in the back of the salon was a great place for deep conversations. One of my employees, Donna May was a lady who was always cheerful. She just seemed to have joy oozing out of every pore in her body. Her happiness was genuine. Donna was very transparent and open about where her joy came from. She talked about God like He was her personal best friend.

During some of my conversations with Donna, my mind wandered back to a place in my childhood memories and I recalled another friend who had talked about God. When I was 10 years old, the house where my family lived was flooded and I had to go live with my friend Diane and her family. They went to church, they prayed and they were kind. Diane's family talked about God, could this be the same God that Donna was talking about?

Donna would sit with me in the back room and share her personal stories about how God had answered many of her prayers. She would use terms that I didn't understand, but her joy and peace were having a deep effect on me. I wanted to learn more about what she had so I could experience it for myself. Eventually she invited me to attend church with her.

On a bright Sunday morning in December, Donna picked me up for church. We drove to Gospel Echoes in Mesa, Arizona and arrived on time for the 10 AM Service. Most of the people I met were just as joyful as Donna was. The service was nice and before it was over, they gave an "altar call." That's the opportunity for folks to come forward and accept Jesus Christ as their personal Lord and Savior. I wasn't ready to do that so I stayed glued to my seat. As we walked back to the car in the parking lot after the service, Donna asked me why I didn't go forward. Almost arrogantly, I haughtily and pridefully replied. "I don't need God in my life! My life is fine!"

Several days later I went to the mall and strangely found myself in a Christian bookstore. It was strange because I had never in my life ever visited a Christian bookstore. I looked around and quickly made the decision to leave. As I turned toward the exit, I noticed a poster on the wall that said, "Behold, I am indelibly imprinted (tattooed a picture of) you on the palm of each of My hands: (O Zion) your walls are continually before Me." It was a quote from the Book of Isaiah 49:16 in the Amplified Bible. The poster showed the hands of God reaching out and it touched my heart. Could it be that God was reaching out for me? I couldn't quite understand what was happening, but my heart was touched in such a way that I began to cry.

I was extremely uncomfortable and almost embarrassed to let anybody see me crying, so I hurried out of the mall. For the next couple of days I couldn't shake the feeling that God was reaching out to me. I was broken and alone, there was no way I could share my innermost feelings with an uncommitted boyfriend. I decided to call Donna and asked to meet with her privately. The salon is always busy and I didn't want other people interrupting our conversation. There was also a small part of me that was afraid to let other people see me cry. Donna graciously invited me to her home.

As I drove to Donna's house, I felt a heavy burden of shame recalling my prideful response to Donna in the church parking lot when I said, "I don't need God in my life!" My feelings of guilt and sadness were almost overwhelming. How could I know the joy and peacefulness that Donna and the other people at church had?

Donna greeted me with her usual smile and hugged me as she invited me inside. I settled into a couch with expectation and yet fearful at the same time. All this God stuff was fairly new to me even though I had first heard about him 21 years earlier. I wanted to explain to Donna what was happening to me. It was almost as if God was trying to get my attention by drawing me toward him. Donna explained to me that God was trying to open up my eyes to the possibility of a greater relationship with him. She said that her life began to change when she accepted Christ into her heart.

Something deep inside my broken spirit told me that I wasn't worthy of love in the way I was living. Donna said that God was knocking on the door of my heart and described how sinfulness is actually a separation from God who is love. She explained why Jesus died on the cross and how his life, death and resurrection revealed God's plan of salvation. Tears welled up inside me as Donna pointed out the truth of what I needed to experience the fullness of God's love.

My brokenness turned into surrender and I laid my life down for God. I prayed and accepted Christ into my heart. Almost immediately my body felt like a dark burden had been lifted off my shoulders. There was a small joy starting to grow in my heart. I was only just beginning to feel the freedom found in the removal of all my guilt and shame. It was like scales had fallen off of my eyes and everything was made new. No longer was I the same person who had walked into Donna's home. My life was new; I now understood how someone can be born again.

The missing ingredient in my life was God. He is a Father who knew me before I was formed in my mother's womb and he knows why he created me and why he created you. God created us to have a relationship of love with him and each other. If there's something missing in your life, try looking for Love, God is love and he is in love with you.

"If we [freely] admit that we have sinned *and* confess our sins, He is faithful and just [true to His own nature and promises], and will forgive our sins and cleanse us *continually* from all unrighteousness [our wrongdoing, everything not in conformity with His will and purpose]"
1 John 1:9 Amplified Bible

CHAPTER TWO

GOD HAS A PERSONAL PLAN

FOR EACH OF US

Now that I knew God was real, I wanted to deepen my personal relationship with Him. I hungered to know what kind of a plan He had for my life. Its one thing to know God, but it's an altogether different thing to follow God. Sitting in a car and knowing how to drive it is not the same as turning the key and putting the car in gear. I wanted to follow God and have his direction in my decision making and in my relationships. I wanted to follow God's plan for my life.

One day while I was at work in the salon, I decided to take a break and go for a walk. There was a man standing outside in the parking lot who smiled and said hello and then began a conversation with me. He told me about a man named Dr. Bill Hamon who was known as a Prophet or someone who could give greater insight into the Truth of God's Word. Bill was going to be speaking at a nearby church and his topic was "God's Plan for People's Lives." I smiled as I thought about this being a timely coincidence or maybe this was an answer from God to my request to know more about His plan for my life.

Several things had changed in my life after I had surrendered my life to Christ. For one thing, I was much more aware of the beauty of God's creation all around me. I noticed small things that I had never paid attention to before. Flowers became extraordinary in their attraction to my senses. Their colors seemed to become more vibrant the longer I stared at them. I went to hear Dr. Hamon speak and was fortunate enough to have him pray for me. The first words out of his mouth as he prayed for me were; "I see you picking flowers!" He gave the analogy of flowers being like people. He said I was like a counselor that would minister to people in need. He said God would use me "to set the captives free."

In the midst of my seeking God's plan for my life, He drew me into His creation through a desire to take a walk on a beautiful day. God planted a man in a parking lot who told me where to go and hear "God's Plan for People's Lives." Through Dr. Bill Hamon, God provided an answer to my request to know His plan for my life.

Also on that evening, a lady who was a member of the Prayer Team gave me a Bible verse. "No good thing will He withhold from those who walk uprightly." She didn't tell me where in the Bible those words could be found. Several days later I was watching a Christian television station. They were requesting donations of canned goods for folks in need. I gathered up two bags of canned goods and drove to the television station.

When I delivered the donations, they invited me to be a part of a television audience. I was excited and eagerly accepted. As I took my seat, the TV cameraman walked over to me and looked me directly in the eye. He spoke with a gentle authority as if delivering a personal message of great importance. He said "Psalm 84:11." That's all he said.

Donna had given me a Bible when I had accepted Christ. Not being sure how to find things in the Bible, I had asked God where to find that verse. I had my Bible with me in the TV studio and looked up Psalm 84:11. It said, "No good thing will He withhold from those who walk uprightly." I smiled and cried as I hugged the Bible to my chest. There was no doubt in my mind that God loved me so much that He took the time to answer me personally. He will answer you personally. Trust him and ask him to come into your heart. Lay out the plans for your life before God and he will lead you and guide you in the way you should go.

"For I know the plans *and* thoughts
that I have for you,'
says the Lord,
'plans for peace *and* well-being
and not for disaster,
to give you a future
and a hope."
Jeremiah 29:11 Amplified Bible

"I will instruct you and teach you
in the way you should go;
I will counsel you
[who are willing to learn]
with My eye upon you."
Psalm 32:8 Amplified Bible

CHAPTER THREE

AN UNKNOWN LANGUAGE

As my hunger for the deeper things of God grew, I began attending church, Bible studies and prayer meetings. Wherever I thought I could gain a greater understanding about the ways of God, that's where I wanted to be.

Donna had weekly Bible studies at her home. On one afternoon after an hour or so of studying the Bible, we began to pray. I was on my knees praying out loud as Donna and I prayed for each other. We also sang worship songs about loving God. During one of those worship songs, I felt something on the tip of my tongue. It was a strange feeling; I could not move whatever it was off the tip of my tongue.

Looking at Donna, I struggled to explain what was happening. Words moved slowly from my mouth as I spoke to her. When I told her that something seemed to be stuck to the tip of my tongue, she placed her hand on my back and told me to just let go. "Release it." She said. "Just open your mouth and release it." She prayed and urged me to let go repeatedly. I opened my mouth and felt my spirit surrender as the words rolled off my tongue. The words sounded like "Santos Mos Dios." I did not know what they meant and I had never spoken them before.

At that point Donna began explaining to me about being baptized in the Holy Spirit and the gift of speaking in tongues. She opened up the Bible to the second Chapter of the Book of Acts and began to read. "When the day of Pentecost came, they were all together in one place. 2 Suddenly a sound like the blowing of a violent wind came from heaven and filled the whole house where they were sitting. 3 They saw what seemed to be tongues of fire that separated and came to rest on each of them. 4 All of them were filled with the Holy Spirit and began to speak in other tongues as the Spirit enabled them."(Acts 2:1-4 New International Version)

Donna explained that the Holy Spirit had baptized me. The words I spoke sounded like Latin words. Though imperfect and not exact, they sounded like words that meant "Most Holy God." After receiving the baptism of the Holy Spirit, I sensed a deeper intimacy with God. I was beginning to understand more about who Jesus was and the magnitude of his sacrifice. I also knew that He was revealing himself to me in a greater measure. Donna explained to me that the more I exercised the gifts that God was giving me, my intimacy with him would grow immeasurably deeper.

Conversations with God grew more frequent in my life after that visitation of the Holy Spirit. I was developing a new spiritual language on a level that I never known before. It became a part of my daily habits to pray to God this way. It was like he was becoming my best friend.

"Oil and perfume
make the heart glad;
So does the sweetness of a friend's counsel
that comes from the heart."
Proverbs 27:9 Amplified Bible

CHAPTER FOUR

THE STILL SMALL VOICE OF GOD

The closer I grew to God through Bible reading, church and especially prayer, I learned more about how to hear his voice. There were things in my life that God wanted removed. They might be small things, but the Bible says that people trusted in small things can be trusted with bigger things. I was in a training ground to hone my listening skills and deepen my communication with the Holy Spirit.

During one of my prayer sessions that was more intense than usual, I heard the Holy Spirit say, "There's idols in the camp." I was familiar with those words as they were similar to the story in seventh chapter of Joshua when Achan had hidden things in his tent that he had stolen after a battle. He had acted deceitfully against the orders that came from God through Joshua. Achan had dishonored God through disobedience and idolatry. He coveted the spoils of war that were supposed to be destroyed.

In my closet was a hand writing analysis that I had done several years ago. Before I had developed a relationship with God, I thought it might be fun to find out what it would reveal about who I was. Now that I had surrendered my life to Christ, looking anywhere but to him would be putting an idol in front of God. He wanted me to remove it, so I tore it up and threw it in the garbage. That may seem like a very small and harmless thing, but the Bible says that "little foxes spoil the vines" Song of Solomon 2:5. God was training me in hearing small things in preparation for greater revelations.

Shopping for bargains in thrift shops is one of my favorite pastimes. During one of my shopping excursions, the Holy Spirit led me to purchase a purse at a used clothing store. I wasn't looking for a purse, but I was drawn to a display case with a selection of purses. I felt strongly moved to purchase an expensive purse that was not my style and not one I would choose to have. The purse was valued at about $200 and I bought it for $40. I took it home and put into my closet and never used it.

Several years later the Lord impressed upon me to give the purse to a teacher in the Bible Study I was attending. After the Bible Study, I approached the teacher carrying a box containing the purse. She smiled as I told her how the Lord had told me to give this to her. She opened the box and excitedly explained that her purse had been stolen a few days earlier. She loved the purse and thanked me for obeying God. I believe that God is simply looking for people to obey him. God can create beautiful surprises from simple acts of obedience and purses from thrift stores!

"And He said, Go out and stand on the mount before the Lord. And behold, the Lord passed by, and a great and strong wind rent the mountains and broke in pieces
the rocks before the Lord,
but the Lord was not in the wind;
and after the wind an earthquake,
but the Lord was not in the earthquake;
And after the earthquake a fire,
but the Lord was not in the fire;
and after the fire
[a sound of gentle stillness and] a still, small voice."
1 Kings 19:11-12 Amplified Bible, Classic Edition

CHAPTER FIVE

I FELL TO THE FLOOR

As my new life in Christ progressed, there was an increase in my experiential relationship with God. The Holy Spirit would touch me in powerful ways during church and Bible meetings. The power of who God was became my new reality in a very intimate way.

During a Tuesday morning Bible Study, we began with worship. The power of God became so strong during worship that I could no longer stand up. No one touched me and no one prayed for me. The Spirit of God touched my innermost being and I was overwhelmed by the presence of God's love. I was in worship and singing the song "As the Deer Panteth for the Water." I was worshiping God in spirit and in truth. Every part of my being was engaged in worship. God had captivated all of me in body and in spirit. I yielded myself totally and yet he had drawn me deeper still by taking me to a place of even greater surrender. I fell to the floor.

Time seemed to pause as I lay in a fetal position on the floor just basking in God's presence. There were no thoughts passing through my mind, only a complete rest in his love. I was in a state of holy peacefulness and just released all of who I was, to all of who he is. The worship that I had entered on my feet became a place of effortless joy as I lay on the floor.

Eventually God released me from the place of complete surrender and I made my way into a chair. Slowly, my body felt relaxed and refreshed like I was waking up from a deep, uninterrupted sleep. My mind was mesmerized by the immensity of God's love and the way he poured it over me so lavishly. I let my body relax in the chair and just soaked in his lingering presence. God is so unbelievably good!

My remembrance of what happened at the Bible Study after that experience is minimal. It's difficult to compose yourself and focus after a life-changing experience. I can only imagine what Moses must have felt after he had seen God's glory on top of the mountain as he received the Ten Commandments. I can only imagine what the Apostle Paul saw on the Road to Damascus that caused him to go blind. I may have been blinded to the rest of the events in that Bible Study because of my experience in God's glory. Opening myself up to worship brought me to a place of greater revelation. My eyes were opened to a greater glimpse of God's personal love.

God is looking for people who are willing to open up and let him move into the center of their lives. Here are the words from Psalm 42:1-2 that paint a beautiful picture of people who pant after him.

"As the deer pants for streams of water,
so my soul pants for you, my God.
My soul thirsts for God, for the living God.
When can I go and meet with God?"

Psalm 42:1-2 New International Version

CHAPTER SIX

SCRATCHED ON MY BIRTHDAY

On July 9, 1996 at 5:30 AM, I was on my way to hike Piestewa Peak in Arizona. It was my birthday and I would begin my special day by hiking up a mountain. My walk with God had progressed to the point where I knew I could pray to him about everything. Some things were more important to me than others, but everything about me is important to God. The Bible says that he even "numbers the hairs on our heads." (Luke 12:7)

On the way to the trailhead I stopped to get gas in my leased Honda Civic. As I pulled away from the gas pumps, I cut the corner a little too close and could feel the car hit something. I stopped and got out to examine my car and saw a big scratch on the side. What a way to start my birthday, by scratching a car that I didn't even own!

The hike up the mountain was good for my scratched ego. I think God allows things in our lives to keep us humble. None of us will ever walk through this world without making mistakes. Pride seems to grow when everything is going well in our lives. My hike was exhilarating, especially when I reached the top in the early morning sunrise. I can't fix a scratch on a car while I'm on top of a mountain so I let it go until a more opportune time.

After I came down from the mountain, I went home to get ready for work. Yes, some of us have to work on our birthdays! I mentioned the scratch on my car to one of my employees. She told me about a company that had done satisfactory work for her. The company was called,

"Colors On Parade." She didn't have their number so I would have to look it up.

This was 1996 and we still used a phone book to find people and companies. There was no listing for Colors On Parade. We didn't use the Internet or Smartphone's to search for companies in those days. Without a phone number or address, there was no way I could find this company. There was only one thing I could do and that was pray. I asked God to help me find that company.

The answer to prayer came as a result of my thirst. After a workout in a local gym, I stopped to get a drink. As I pulled into the store parking lot, a truck pulled up next to my car. Written on the side of the truck were the words, "Colors On Parade." I smiled at God's timing and answer to my prayers. I jumped out and almost startled the driver of the truck as excitedly exclaimed, "O my gosh, I've been looking for you!" I asked for his card so that I could call him later and make an appointment. Soon thereafter, my scratched car looked like new as they did an excellent job.

This may be a small story, but God cares for all of our needs. big or small, he answers – always. We will have small struggles and big struggles; God uses the small struggles as training grounds to help teach us the value of praying in all circumstances.

"Be unceasing and persistent in prayer;
in every situation
[no matter what the circumstances]
be thankful and continually give thanks to God;
for this is the will of God for you in Christ Jesus."
1 Thessalonians 5:17-18 Amplified Bible

CHAPTER SEVEN

A SIGN OF CONFIRMATION

Early one Tuesday morning I left home and drove to my salon to get ready for an 8 AM appointment. Just as I drove around the first block in the townhouse complex in which I lived, I spotted a for sale sign. I wasn't really looking to move, but I'm always curious what homes are selling for in my neighborhood. You never know when an opportunity to upgrade will come along so it's good to be prepared. I stopped my car and copied down the phone number from the for sale sign.

Arriving at the salon at 7:30 AM gave me a few minutes to call the number from the sign. The phone rang a few times before the answering machine came on. I still remember what it said, "Roses are red, violets are blue, leave a message. You know what to do!" I smiled as I replied to the machine and said I was calling about the townhouse for sale. After that it was time to prepare for my first appointment of the day.

After completing a good day at work, I drove home around 3:30 PM. As I rounded the corner on the last block near my home, I noticed that the for sale sign was missing. It really didn't matter that much to me as I was only seeking information anyway. That was on Tuesday afternoon and the whole episode began to fade from my mind. I would have totally forgotten the sign if not for what happened on Thursday evening.

It was about 9:30 PM Thursday evening and I was lying on my bed watching TV. I like to wind down and end my day by relaxing with a nature show. My eyes were just about to close when the phone rang. In those days we didn't have cell phones and my phone was across the room and I would have to get up out of bed to answer it. I was a bit annoyed, (actually I was very annoyed!) I almost ignored it and let it ring, but something inside me made me get up and answer the phone.

The lady on the other end of the line identified herself and asked if I was the one who had called about the townhouse for sale. I replied that I was and was about to ask her if she knew how late it was for making phone calls, but I withheld my grumpiness. She asked me where I had seen the for sale sign. I told her that on Tuesday morning about 7 AM, I had seen the sign in my neighborhood and when I came home around 3:30 PM the same day it was gone. She then asked where I lived. I told her I was in Quails Landing in Phoenix. She continued asking questions and I tried to be patient in my sleepiness. She asked if it was possible if I had seen the sign in Mesa where she lived. I said "No, I'm positive it was right here in my neighborhood. I drove to my salon and arrived at 7:30 AM that morning."

The next question caught me off guard a little and made me listen with increasing attentiveness. "Would you by any chance happen to be a Christian?" Her voice began to waver like someone being overcome emotionally. In the midst of hearing my own voice tell her that I was a Christian, the sound of her crying also reached my ears. I paused and waited to see what she would say next. Something was happening and my spirit was sensing that God had something to do with it.

The woman went on to explain that she felt like the Holy Spirit was telling her to sell her townhouse. She wanted to make sure that it was really God so she asked Him for a sign. My phone call about a for sale sign that she never put up was her confirmation and a sign from God. She never put up a sign. She lived over 30 miles away from me. The sign disappeared. We both agreed that God had indeed planted and uprooted a sign in answer to her prayer.

God answers prayers in many different ways. Sometimes he will confirm an answer to our questions through people, circumstances, prayer and the Bible. It's good to be patient and sure in seeking answers from God. His Word says to "Be still and know."

Psalm 46 Amplified Bible
"God is our refuge and strength [mighty and impenetrable],
A very present *and* well-proved help in trouble.
Therefore we will not fear, though the earth should change
And though the mountains be shaken *and* slip into the heart of the seas, Though its waters roar and foam,
Though the mountains tremble at its roaring. *Selah.*

There is a river whose streams make glad the city of God,
The holy dwelling places of the Most High.
God is in the midst of her [His city], she will not be moved;
God will help her when the morning dawns.
The nations made an uproar, the kingdoms tottered *and* were moved; He raised His voice, the earth melted. The LORD of hosts is with us; The God of Jacob is our stronghold [our refuge, our high tower]. *Selah.*

Come, behold the works of the LORD,
Who has brought desolations *and* wonders on the earth.
He makes wars to cease to the end of the earth;
He breaks the bow into pieces and snaps the spear in two;
He burns the chariots with fire.
"Be still and know (recognize, understand) that I am God.
I will be exalted among the nations! I will be exalted in the earth." The LORD of hosts is with us; The God of Jacob is our stronghold [our refuge, our high tower]. *Selah."*

CHAPTER EIGHT

HE JUST WANTS TO HEAR OUR VOICE

Time spent with God has a wonderful way of becoming a deep pool of refreshing understanding and discernment. I loved my prayer time with God. Looking back on it now, my personal prayer time with Him was both a time of personal growth and a training ground for greater opportunities yet to come.

A friend of mine invited me to visit the church he was attending. During the service, I felt the Holy Spirit tell me it was okay to leave now. I got up and left immediately. I walked to my car as the tears began to flow. Crying, I sat there in the parking lot for a few minutes. There was a strong feeling inside me that something wasn't right; I cried all the way home. As soon as I walked in the door, I got down on my knees and began to pray. I asked God what was making me so uncomfortable about that church. Through my tears he spoke one word, "exploit." Something in the church was contrary to the Truth of God and people were being exploited.

Eventually God closed the doors of that church. I don't know the particular reasons why, other than the one word that God had given me, "exploit." Whatever did happen caused people to get hurt. My friend was one of those people who got hurt when the church closed. After that experience and because he knew the Holy Spirit had alerted me to the problems, my friend began to trust me and my relationship with God. That trust opened up a whole new opportunity to pray for him. God was now expanding my prayer life to include praying for other people.

Soon thereafter, during a conversation about prayer, a friend of mine was questioning the need to pray to God so often. He was frustrated by things in his life and thought he shouldn't have to keep repeating himself to God. I heard the Lord reveal to me the reason for persistent prayer was motivated by nothing more than his pure love. The reason he wants us to pray so often is just to hear our voice. The Holy Spirit said to me, "I just love to hear your voice." His words were so gentle, kind and powerful in providing a perfect answer to my friend's question. They also gave me a humble patience as I continued to pray with my friend.

Once again, I began to cry. A word of knowledge directly from God overwhelms me to the point of tears. It's almost like my heart is suddenly filled to overflowing with his overpowering Love. As I explained all these things to my friend, I believe his anger at God began to soften. All of us need to grow and it takes time. We all need to be patient with each other.

The Bible says to pray with perseverance and persistence. Prayer sharpens our alertness to people, places and things that aren't in line with God's way of love. I would encourage you to keep on praying and be alert for his voice. He loves to hear yours!

"With all prayer and petition pray [with specific requests] at all times [on every occasion and in every season] in the Spirit, and with this in view, stay alert with all perseverance and petition [interceding in prayer] for all God's people." Ephesians 6:18 Amplified Bible

"Be persistent and devoted to prayer, being alert and focused in your prayer life with an attitude of thanksgiving." Colossians 4:2 Amplified Bible

CHAPTER NINE

TAKING OUR GREY AREAS TO GOD

Repentance is a big word that's often misunderstood. Its basic meaning is that someone is admitting their sorrow over sinning against God and they seek his forgiveness and help in changing their habits. Sometimes our sin is very apparent and there's no doubt that we've done something morally wrong. Other times we enter into grey areas where we're not sure if we've sinned or not. I was in a grey area so I prayed and asked God about it. I wanted a clean heart so I left no possible sin unturned.

Over the course of my journey with God, he had given me many opportunities to help people. I was grateful for the ability to make a difference in people's lives. God would point the way, point out the people and allow me to be used by him. Helping people is a beautiful experience that almost provides its own gratitude, even if folks never say thank you. At least that's what I told myself. Still, there was a nagging feeling in my gut that it would be nice for someone to express gratitude. Couldn't at least one of these people say "thank you?"

The gnawing desire for gratitude was very unsettling. I started to wonder if my attitude was wrong. I wasn't supposed to do things for people with an expectation of receiving anything in return, but I knew that saying thank you was just a common courtesy. Was my desire to be recognized as someone who was being helpful a wrong attitude? Was I wrong in expecting folks to express gratitude? Was my attitude a sin?

Pouring my heart out to God, I expressed my desire to be used by him continually. I asked him to create in me a clean heart and show me anything in me that was contrary to the way he wanted me to live. I was at peace with my prayer and the gnawing feeling in my gut started to melt away. Three days after that session of prayer, I received three thank you notes in the mail. All of them expressed the gratitude that I had been thirsting for. One of the notes was from someone I had helped a fairly long time ago. Once again I felt tears well up in my eyes.

God knows our hearts and he knows our intentions. He knows the smallest thoughts that we have. Being intimate with God is being totally transparent. That's the way trusting relationships are built to last. God honors our honesty with him, he will bring to pass anything that will help us grow closer to him. All thoughts big or small, the Lord God loves them all! I know that sounds like a borrowed cliché, but it definitely describes what I learned about sharing my grey areas with God. There are things that I can do that are acceptable, but I want to do the things that are beneficial to my relationship with God.

"All things are lawful
[that is, morally legitimate, permissible],
but not all things are beneficial
or advantageous.
All things are lawful,
but not all things are constructive
[to character]
and edifying [to spiritual life].
Let no one seek [only] his own good,
but [also] that of the other person."

1 Corinthians 10:23-24 Amplified Bible

CHAPTER TEN

BEAUTY FOR ASHES

Songs of praise and worship can help create beautiful moments where God's Love is like a symphony in my soul. His peace descends on me like an autumn leaf falling slowly earthward in the season of fall. Being in a worship experience is one of my favorite things to do. I've found that the presence of God seems to linger even after the worship music fades.

In January, 1989, my friend and I attended a Leon Patillo Concert in Mesa, Arizona. Leon is the former lead singer for the rock band Santana. He left the band to pursue a path where he could sing and preach about God and his Love. We enjoyed Leon's concert immensely and I felt touched by the Holy Spirit. I can't remember what Leon said or even the songs that he sang, but that doesn't matter. All that matters is that I recall being at an event where God's presence was real. It was so real that I carried it with me for several days.

When I got home, the worship music was still playing inside my mind. I laid down on my bed, still feeling that overwhelming peace that transcends all understanding. Something different was happening that I had never experienced before. I could feel physical changes within my body. Deep inside me, in my inner being, I could feel warmth spreading all over me. It was like warm oil or honey was seeping into my veins and flowing outward from my heart. In my spirit I knew it was God's Love.

Worship is an act of praise that's like a crescendo rising in intensity until it reaches the summit of God. The climax comes down like a multi-colored leaf falling in its last act of total surrender. The wind that carries the leaf is like the breath of a still small voice that says, "I love you." I was feeling that fullness of God's love flow through every fiber of my being as I drifted off to sleep. I slept in peace.

In the morning I wondered if what happened to me was real or just a dream. Any notion regarding the reality of my experience was quickly dispelled by the way I still felt. Deep within me that feeling of love was still percolating through my veins. Everywhere I went for the next few days, my heart beheld a powerful love for everyone I met. I smiled and felt like I must be glowing with God's goodness. It didn't matter what they said or how they acted, I only desired that they could experience the enormity of God's Love. I wanted God to touch them as he had touched me. At work in my salon, I looked at the employees and clients the same way.

Gradually, like the leaf that eventually hits the ground, God relaxed his hold on me. I believe God gives us a break from the intensity of his love. Seasons change for the simple reason in that there is a unique beauty in all seasons. From the bursting colors of summer blooms, to the brilliant colors of falling leaves, to the bleakness of frozen winter nights, to the budding new beginnings of spring, God loves us in all seasons from our deepest lows to our highest highs. He tarries in one season until we are ready for the new season that is just about to begin.

Seeing how God loves me in different seasons helped get me ready for the seasons of heartbreak that lay in front of me. I didn't know it then, but God was preparing me to go through brokenness. Because of that experience, I came to understand that through brokenness we are given a greater capacity to love.

"He has sent me
to announce the time when the Lord
will show his kindness
and the time when our God
will punish evil people.
He has sent me
to comfort all those who are sad.
He has sent me
to the sorrowing people of Jerusalem.
I will give them a crown
to replace their ashes.
I will give them the oil of gladness
to replace their sorrow.
I will give them clothes of praise
to replace their spirit of sadness.
Then they will be called Trees of Goodness.
They will be like trees planted by the Lord
and will show his greatness."

Isaiah 61:2-3 International Children's Bible

CHAPTER ELEVEN

GOD USES OUR FAITH TO COVER MISTAKES

An adult who acts like a child in the eyes of God is a beautiful picture of humble faith. Our lives are like journeys that traverse over mountains of joy and valleys of sorrow. Sometimes God covers our mistakes as a way of rewarding and rejuvenating our faith in him. Children have an innocence and believe what they are told more readily. God desires that we have childlike faith in him.

My partner and I were opening up a brand new salon. The building was in a plaza and we were responsible for all of the construction inside the shell of a building. The whole interior structure was being prepared especially for us from the ground up. Our grand opening was already being delayed due to construction setbacks and management decisions. Things finally progressed to the point where we could schedule a firm date for our grand opening.

As the salon manager, I was responsible for many things and it became a bit overwhelming. One of my responsibilities was scheduling the electric company to come and turn our electric on. In the busyness, I forgot to call the electric company ahead of time.

When I finally made the call, it was the afternoon before the grand opening. They said it was impossible to schedule a work crew to come out and turn on our electric before 8 AM on such short notice. I pleaded with them and explained our situation. The best they could do is put our salon last on their schedule for the next day which meant approximately 3:30 PM. We already had clients scheduled for 8 AM.

Going to a private place, I went to pray and asked God for help with my problem. After I was done praying, my whole body was flooded with peace. I firmly believed and had faith that everything would be okay. I slept peacefully that night.

My partner was slightly irritated by my failure to act responsibly. I knew I had let her down, but I assured her that I believed God had answered my prayer and that everything would turn out well. Still, she made contingency plans. The landlord of the building was allowing us to use his generator to provide electricity. My partner had placed extension cords all over the place so that each station in the salon would have access to electricity.

On the day of our grand opening, we arrived around 7 AM to get ready for our first appointment at 8 AM. At approximately 7:30 AM, a power company truck pulled up in the back of the salon. One of the workers said they were there to turn the electricity on. I smiled as asked him, "I thought they put us last on your schedule?" The man replied, "No mam, we have you as first on the schedule."

We had electricity buzzing away before our first client arrived. My partner was happy, but also felt a little embarrassed at her lack of faith. I assured her she did nothing wrong, it was me who God had called to have faith. After all, it was my mistake in the first place. Faith grows in many ways. We will make mistakes in life, many mistakes, but God can make our mistakes work together for good when we have faith in him.

"Jesus looked at them and said, "For men this is impossible. But for God all things are possible." Many who are first now will be last in the future. And many who are last now will be first in the future."
Matthew 19:26,30 International Children's Bible

CHAPTER TWELVE

TIGGER UNDER THE ANGEL TREE

Christmas is a wonderful season that brings out a contagious giving spirit in folks. Most people find more joy in giving than they do in receiving. The Bible says that "God loves a cheerful giver." (2 Corinthians 9:7) God also expects us to give our best effort and the best gift that we have the ability to give. Sometimes our best that God asks us to give is something that's very dear to us.

Every year at East Valley Assembly of God, they put up an Angel Tree just after Thanksgiving. Monty and Kelly Sears were the Lead Pastors and their giving hearts had a deep effect on untold numbers of people. The Angel Tree could also be called a "giving tree" or an "opportunity tree." The tree provided an opportunity for folks to become secret angels and give presents to kids who might not otherwise receive any gifts during the Christmas season. The Angel Tree provided a beautiful experience for both givers and receivers.

The children would write a note detailing what kind of present they would like for Christmas. I went to the tree and retrieved a card from its branches. It was a note from a little girl who was about eight years old. She wrote a sweet message requesting a "Tigger," who's a character from Winnie The Pooh. Tigger is a bouncing, always happy, slightly irresponsible tiger, who just happened to be one of my favorites. I had been collecting Tigger figures for several years. This was an exciting coincidence or better yet, this was a God-incidence! I was about to anonymously share my love for collecting Tiggers with a little girl.

In my Tigger collection, I had a favorite. It was a bouncing Tigger that talked and said, "I've got a lot of bouncing to do!" This particular stuffed Tigger had been given to me by a little boy next door to where I lived. It was my favorite Tigger and part of a great memory. In the midst of wondering what I would get as a Tigger gift for the little girl, the Holy Spirit whispered to me "Give her your best. Give her your favorite Tigger." God has a way of introducing conflict into our giving seasons. I didn't want to give up my best and favorite Tigger!

At first I hoped that I had made a mistake in my hearing and even considered pleading with God when I knew what he was asking of me. He wanted me to give my best because he gives us his best. I relented and wrapped up my favorite Tigger, pulling the last bit of wrapping paper over the little tiger very slowly, taking one last glance at his happy face. Finished, I taped the little girls note to the wrapped present and put it under the Angel Tree. I can only imagine the smile on the little girl's face as she opened her gift. I was happy; I had given my best, even though I struggled a bit in the process.

A short time later, I was walking into my salon to get ready for another full day of appointments. I gasped in surprise and was shocked as a great big smile creased my face when I spotted what was in my salon chair. There was a great big Tigger that took up the whole chair! Everyone began laughing in the salon as they saw the look on my face. One of the girls explained where this big Tigger had come from. She was at a friend's house and saw a Tigger in the corner of the garage and thought of me. She asked the man about it and he said he would be happy give it to her.

The small Tigger had been my best and God had asked me to give it away. I obeyed and in return God had given me his best in the form of a huge Tigger. In the big picture of our lives, there are more important things than stuffed animals, but God can use anything to help us grow our faith. Introducing conflict in the middle of gift giving may seem strange, but the fact is nothing grows without conflict.

When you find yourself between a rock and a hard place, trust God and he will bring rivers of living water out of the rock! Life has a way of coming full circle, what you give will come back to you in greater measure.

Now [remember] this:
he who sows sparingly will also reap sparingly,
and he who sows generously
[that blessings may come to others]
will also reap generously [and be blessed].
Let each one give [thoughtfully and with purpose]
just as he has decided in his heart, not grudgingly or under
compulsion, for God loves a cheerful giver [and delights in the
one whose heart is in his gift].
2 Corinthians 9:6-7 Amplified Bible

CHAPTER THIRTEEN

CHRISTMAS SHOEBOXES FOR CHILDREN

After moving into my townhouse, I threw out all of the moving boxes. Trying to reduce any unneeded clutter, everything that I had no reason to keep, went into the dumpster. Little did I know that some of those boxes I threw out, could have been useful in helping needy children.

The Mountain Park Church in Ahwatukee, Arizona participated in Operation Christmas Child every year. I received newsletters in the mail from the Billy Graham Association and that's where I heard about Operation Christmas Child. The Project is administered by Samaritan's Purse to minister to children in war torn and famine stricken countries around the world. I love Christmas and I like to buy gifts. Filling a shoebox with gifts for needy boys and girls touched my heart. It was one of my Christmas customs that brought a deep sense of fulfillment. Lives are changed by the power of Christ through the gift of giving.

Finding a shoebox had never been a problem for me. There are many shoes in my closets and storing them in the original box keeps them in good condition. For some strange reason, there were no shoeboxes in my closet. I suppose it's possible that I was a bit overzealous in cleaning up the clutter from moving, and I must have thrown them all away. I had the heart to give, but now I was missing the shoebox!

In search of a shoebox, I asked my neighbors, friends and the employees in my salon, but nobody had a shoebox. I thought it was strange that nobody had an extra shoebox lying around. Frustrated, there was only one place left to turn, so I prayed and asked God for help. Praying for God to give me a shoebox may seem strange to some folks, but he cares about everything in our lives. God wants to hear from us in big things and little things. He wants to hear about our joys and problems. He also wants to hear us say, "Thank you." And "I love you." I did say those things and then I asked for help finding one shoebox.

About two days later I was at home and felt a strong urge to go out to the recycle bins. I did have a few items to take out, so I gathered them up and headed out the door. Walking across the parking lot, I was halfway to the recycling area when I lifted my head and looked in the direction of the bins. There on the top of a recycle bin, were six shoeboxes neatly stacked one on top of the other. There were two stacks of three shoeboxes piled side by side. I stopped dead in my tracks and stared in almost unbelief. God had answered my prayers for one shoebox by providing me with six shoeboxes! I tossed the recyclables from my hands into another bin and scooped up the shoeboxes. The joy within me welled up and burst out as I laughed and yelled, "Thank you Jesus!" Looking back on it now, I believe the Holy Spirit was leading me to go out to those recycle bins with perfect timing.

So now I had to fill six shoeboxes instead of one. It wasn't what I expected, but you could say that the joy I received from filling one Christmas Shoebox was multiplied six times! With a smile on my face and a smile in my heart, I drove to the dollar store. Buying items for three girls and three boys was a lot of fun. I tried to imagine the smiles on the children's faces as they opened their shoebox full of gifts.

Operation Christmas Child is the culmination of many people doing small things that add up to an unbelievably huge blessing. Since 1993, Samaritan's Purse has delivered 157

Million Operation Christmas Child Shoebox Gifts to children in need in 160 countries. These shoeboxes are a way to share the gospel through an act of love in the name of Christ. Small acts of love can make an eternal impact.

Now to Him who is able to
[carry out His purpose and]
do superabundantly more than
all that we dare ask or think
[infinitely beyond our greatest prayers, hopes, or dreams],
according to His power that is at work within us,
to Him be the glory in the church
and in Christ Jesus
throughout all generations forever and ever.
Amen.
Ephesians 3:20-21 Amplified Bible

CHAPTER FOURTEEN

THE TRUTH WILL SET YOU FREE

Most folks desire deep interpersonal relationships that explore the possibility of a potential marriage. Three years can be a long time, but time will give you a fairly accurate glimpse into the real heart of a person. My boyfriend and I had discussed marriage, and at one point it seemed like a real possibility. Still, I didn't have real peace in the relationship. I felt that maybe the Holy Spirit was holding me back and had other plans for me.

Toward the end of the three years, we began having discussions about either "tying the knot" or breaking up and going our separate ways. We did have closeness between us, but there was still an uneasy feeling. Trust was a big issue with me, I knew what it was like to be hurt by someone you love.

After one of our discussions about our future, it seemed inevitable that we would be splitting up. I asked my boyfriend if he was already seeing someone else. He emphatically responded "No!" There was still a slim thread that bound us together and a glimmer of hope that we could work things out. I left him that day thinking that I really had to spend time with God and seek his direction.

Many times when I wanted to spend time with God, I would go for a hike in the mountains near my home. South Mountain Park is the largest municipal park in the United States and one of the largest urban parks in the world. Despite the number of people who visited the park, the sheer vastness of the area provided many opportunities for solitude. I had a special place I called my "prayer rock." I would hike up to the rock and pray with my Bible.

My last discussion with my boyfriend happened on a Monday evening. I'm full of energy early in the morning and often head for the mountains around 6 AM. On that particular Tuesday, my first appointment at the salon was at 8 AM. After I had finished meeting with all of my scheduled clients, I went home and decided to go climb a mountain. South Mountain is close enough to my home that I would walk there and still have plenty of time for an afternoon hike.

Strapping on my backpack, I laced up my hiking shoes, grabbed a hiking stick, a few bottles of water and headed for the mountain. Prayer rock was my one and only focus and sole destination. Reaching the rock, I poured out my heart to God. I surrendered my relationship to him and asked for his guidance in making a decision. My question to God was simple, "Should I stay or should I go?" He didn't give me any exact directions concerning the relationship with my boyfriend, but it didn't matter. I had the feeling for several months that God wanted me to sever the relationship.

Even though I hadn't received an exact answer to my question, I did feel peace deep down inside. Something was happening and I would just have to be patient. The Bible says "To be still and know that I am God." (Psalm 46:10) After returning home from the mountain, I got ready to leave for an evening Bible Study with some friends. The Study at Grace Community Church lasted from 7 PM – 8:30 PM.

On the way home, I usually travelled over the main roads and avoided the expressways. For some reason I decided on this night to take the expressways. Sometimes there are decisions we make that we don't quite understand until later. We may call it leading with our intuition or gut feeling, but I believe that God is giving us a "heads-up" to where his Holy Spirit will lead us. I merged onto the turnpike and blended into the moderate evening traffic.

After only a few miles, my boyfriend's truck suddenly crossed over in front of me. He was travelling a bit faster, so I pushed down on the gas pedal to catch up with him, I could feel the butterflies beginning to unsettle my stomach. He wasn't alone. This was no coincidence; we had just talked about him seeing someone else and now the truth was being revealed right in front of me. As I pulled up behind him, I could see very clearly that his passenger was a woman who was sitting very close to him. My heart sank as I felt the sting of betrayal and rejection. I had asked him if he was seeing someone and he had lied to me.

My car pulled in behind him at the apartment complex where he lived. My former boyfriend got out of his truck as his close companion remained seated. I rolled down my window and asked him one question, "Why didn't you tell me the truth?" His answer in defense of his lie was, "You can't handle the truth!" There's some sad humor in his response. That's a quote from a movie called "A Few Good Men" during an investigation into the death of a soldier. Our relationship was now dead and the lie was over.

Betrayal, rejection and lies will always be hurtful and leave emotional scars. However, God allows episodes of pain in our lives so we can develop greater compassion. It can be challenging when you're trying to help folks walk through trials if you haven't walked in their shoes. Brokenness given to God often results in the growth of compassion and empathy in our hearts.

"Then you will know
the truth.
And the truth
will make you free."

John 8:32 International Children's Bible

CHAPTER FIFTEEN

MY BEST FRIEND

After I severed all ties with my boyfriend, my heart was drawn deeper into a relationship with Christ. I didn't know it at the time, but this was the beginning of a five year period of being alone with God. There would not be any romantic relationships with man. Sometimes I would get lonely, but the Holy Spirit always seemed to send somebody to let me know how special I was.

It might sound kind of peculiar, but in a spiritual way, God became my best friend. Instead of being on a date with a man, I would spend my time in prayer, worship, studying the Bible and hiking in the mountains. I would take many hikes up to my special "prayer rock" and spend countless hours in prayer. Fulfilled as I was, there were times when I missed the closeness I had felt in a relationship. My 45th birthday was one of those times.

It was around noon after I'd gone for a hike and I was hungry. Safeway is a great store to find some healthy food for a hungry and lonely soul. I grabbed a shopping cart and moved quickly toward the produce aisle. I had my mind set on this being a quick trip. I would just get what I needed and head home to eat. Then a man tried to strike up a conversation.

I had noticed him looking at me as I grabbed a container of baby spinach. He pushed his cart up alongside mine and asked me if I hiked or worked out. He said it was easy to see that I was in great physical shape. I didn't want a conversation, but I talked with him for a few minutes. I told him that I did work out at the gym and I also liked to go hiking. His favorite pastime was playing golf. He was a nice man, but at this point in my life, I had no interest in dating anybody. After a few minutes of pleasant chatter, we went our separate ways.

It was my birthday and I was going home alone. Spending time with God is a beautiful thing and I'm happy to do that. Every once in awhile though, I longed for those things you receive when you're in a relationship. On birthdays, it's a foregone conclusion that you will receive a gift of some sort from the person you're dating. There was a part of me that desired to be remembered with a gift.

I loaded the groceries into the trunk of my car and shut the lid. As I turned to take the shopping cart back, I saw the man who liked golf standing right next to my car. He just smiled and handed me a bouquet of flowers. He said that he put his business card inside the bouquet and that if I ever wanted a free golf lesson to give him a call. He said that he had never done anything like this before and was surprised that he was even doing it. I thanked him and that was the last time I ever saw him.

I cried as I sat inside my car. I knew that God had remembered me on my birthday. There was no doubt in my mind that these flowers were a gift from the Holy Spirit. He knew my thoughts. He knew how lonely I felt. He knew how I longed to be remembered by somebody. His message to me spoke loud and clear, "I can supply all of your needs." Many years later, I still have those flowers, sealed and preserved.

It would be five years before I felt released to reenter the dating scene. They passed quickly and my longing for man decreased as my longing for God increased. As I got to know God more, he taught me how to bring relationships to him in order to reveal the truth of what was in a man's heart. Some folks remain single, some become widowed or divorced and some folks will get married, God will guide you in all relationships.

"The Lord is my best friend and my shepherd.
I always have more than enough.
He offers a resting place for me
in his luxurious love.
His tracks take me to an oasis of peace,
the quiet brook of bliss.
That's where he restores and revives my life.
He opens before me
pathways to God's pleasure
and leads me along in his footsteps of righteousness
so that I can bring honor to his name.
Lord, even when your path takes me through
the valley of deepest darkness,
fear will never conquer me,
for you already have!
You remain close to me
and lead me through it all the way.
Your authority is my strength and my peace.
The comfort of your love takes away my fear.
I'll never be lonely, for you are near."
Psalm 23:1-4 The Passion Translation

"God, all at once
You turned on a floodlight for me!
You are the revelation-light
in my darkness,
and in your brightness
I can see the path ahead."
Psalm 18:28 The Passion Translation

CHAPTER SIXTEEN

PRAYER TURNED UPSIDE DOWN

There are many things in life that tend to defy logic and common sense. Not everything we see will be used for the way we think it will. God has a way of turning our lives upside down as his way of putting things in their right place. He has an exact way of doing things and he also desires that we are specific in our prayer requests.

Interior decorating in my own home is something I love to do. When friends give me gifts that I can hang on my walls, I take great pleasure in exploring different areas of my home where I could display them. I was home one afternoon looking at my collection of moose figurines. Friends and clients had given me humorous little moose figures over a period of years, and now they had grown into a nice little collection. I wanted to put them all on a shelf, but I didn't have one.

By now, you've probably figured out that I like to try and pray about the smallest of decisions and desires. I prayed and asked God for a shelf. As I prayed, I heard the Holy Spirit say "Be specific." I sat for a few moments and pondered what kind of shelf I would like in terms of style and color. What came to my mind was a teakwood shelf with black trim. Teakwood is well known for its quality and tends to be a golden or medium brown that darkens over time. I asked God for a teakwood shelf for my collection of moose's.

Stein Mart is a great store where I would find many high value items at discounted prices. As I was shopping, I felt a strong pull toward a display of office organizers. I picked one up and just felt like I was supposed to buy it, figuring that maybe God was telling me to be more organized. That I could understand, all of us could use a bit more organization in our lives. I made the purchase of the office organizer and left the store. My search for a teak wood moose shelf would have to wait for another day.

When I arrived at home, I took the office organizer inside and set it on my desk. It didn't take a lot of common sense or logic to figure that out. I took the packaging off and held it in my hands. I can only give God credit for what happened next. The thought entered my mind to take the office organizer, turn it upside down and hold it up against the wall. So I followed my thoughts, turned it over and held it up to the wall. There before my eyes, the upside down office organizer transformed into a perfect teak wood shelf with black trim! I was astounded and amazed to say the least!

God had answered my specific prayer in a way that defied logic. He took an office organizer with a specific purpose and changed its intended purpose. The Holy Spirit was teaching me to be specific and clear in my prayers. He was also teaching me to lean into him with a greater awareness of how he can use all things for a greater purpose.

There were several good lessons that I came away with from my "Moose Shelf Prayer." The more I look back on that experience; it evolves into an adventure in learning God's greater ways. Prayers for small things can help me glean heart nuggets that contain large amounts of wisdom. It's good to be clear in our communication in all relationships. All of us hear and understand things through our own unique life experience. Communicating clearly includes making sure the other person understands exactly what you intend them to understand.

Turning life upside down is often the method that God uses to create a more excellent way. Using a pagan form of execution to crucify his Son defies logic and common sense.

Jesus died to pay the price for the times that we failed to show love to God and people. There are consequences for wrong actions. That's common sense, but God turned death upside down when Jesus was resurrected. As we believe in him, we gain new life.

"Go ahead and make all the plans you want,
but it's the Lord
who will ultimately direct your steps.
We are all in love with our own opinions,
convinced they're correct.
But the Lord
is in the midst of us,
testing and probing our every motive.
Before you do anything,
put your trust totally in God
and not in yourself.
Then every plan you make
will succeed."

Proverbs 16:1-3 The Passion Translation

CHAPTER SEVENTEEN

A STILL SMALL VOICE

AND

THE JOY OF LAUGHTER

Life has many wilderness trails that may seem lonely until we experience God in the middle of nowhere. Sometimes he will even take us down dead-end roads to help teach us a lesson. The Holy Spirit touches us in many ways as he uses the natural things around us to reveal his supernatural nature. He can teach us through a magnificent sunrise or a miniature pebble of sand by the seashore. He can also touch us by placing odd things in odd places.

We had great working relationships in our salon. Some clients would come to me to get their hair done and then would go to our Nail Technician to get their nails done. Barbara was one of those clients who took advantage of all the services our salon had to offer. After a recent trip to Disneyland in California, Barbara brought back a Mickey Mouse ball and had given it to Sally our Nail Tech. I laughed as I first saw the antenna topper ball sitting on Sally's Manicure Table. My first response was like the reaction of a small child, "Mickey Mouse! I'd like to have one of those!"

Sometimes we see things and express a desire to have them, but they're not placed very high on our priority list. Most of the time, small episodes like this fade from our memories because of their lack of importance in our lives. I wasn't focused on going out and searching for my own Mickey Mouse ball. When I was growing up on Staten Island in New York, I often heard the adults say, "In the grand scheme of things, I've got bigger fish to fry!" That pretty much described my thoughts about a Mickey Mouse ball. I believe that life has a way of letting us know what's really important.

Several days later I went hiking in South Mountain Park. It was early on a Sunday morning, about 6 AM and a few hours before I would go to church. South Mountain was my favorite place to get away for some peaceful time with God. I would hike there at least five days per week, and sometimes even more. I did have favorite trails and my special places like the one I call "Prayer Rock." Sometimes I would just go "as the Spirit leads me." What I mean by that is, I would follow my "gut feeling" or my intuition. The deeper my relationship with God grew; I knew he was guiding me whenever I allowed my spirit to be surrendered to him. You may have felt "urgings" to do things in your own life. Sometimes it seems like a "still, small voice," and other times it's like "a mighty rushing wind." We can be pushed and pulled by our opinions and the opinions of people around us, but God will point the way when we allow him to.

I stopped to have a drink of water and take a few bites from the energy bar I had packed for my trail breakfast. I was at the junction of two trails and hadn't made up my mind which trail I would follow. I got up from the rock on which I was sitting, and packed away my water bottle. Standing there, I looked around and took in the beauty of God's creation that surrounded me. The sky was an incredibly cloudless blue as far as my eyes could see. Giant saguaros and other forms of cactus covered the sides of rocky mountain peaks that stretched into the sky. I took a deep breath and felt an "intuitive-nudge" to take the trail on my left. With my walking stick leading the way, up the trail I went.

After ascending many switchbacks, or the twists and turns on the trail, it was time for another water and food break. Switchbacks are cut into the trail mostly so that when it does rain, the water doesn't become a flood and rush straight down the mountain. A trail that leads straight up the mountain is harder to maintain because rain can wash away dirt, rocks and almost anything in its path. God often takes us on switchback trails so we can walk more slowly and see things we may not see if we charged through life full speed ahead.

Looking around for the most comfortable rock to rest on, something strange caught my eye. When you've hiked in the mountains for as many times as I have, your eyes become conditioned to the colors that are a part of that natural landscape. Strange colors in the mountain landscape stand out like a guy wearing a bathing suit in a Buffalo blizzard! I walked toward the strange colors and almost tripped over some rocks as I started laughing. It was a Mickey Mouse ball! Here I was in the middle of nowhere, in the wilderness, and I found a Mickey Mouse ball!

My laughter soon turned to crying as I sat on a rock with the ball in my hands. I didn't pray for this to happen, but God wanted me to have some joy. He is a God who turns mourning into dancing and ashes into beauty. Sometimes God does little things to let us know how important we are to him. The Bible says he's numbered the hairs on our heads. That's another way of saying, he knows every thought in our minds and every desire buried deeply within our hearts. He brings moments of joy so that we can remember them in times of trial. He will never leave us or forsake us. He's a God of the trivial and the God of the tremendous!

One final note before I close this chapter. There was one friend of mine who thought this story was nothing but a frivolous coincidence. She called me foolish for believing that God would somehow arrange for a Mickey Mouse ball to suddenly appear on a mountain trail just for me. I'm perfectly okay with being called foolish.

The more I know God, the more I realize how much he cares about every detail in our lives being worked into something good. Every detail includes finding antenna topper balls on mountain peaks!

"God said,
"Go out and stand in front of the Lord
on the mountain."
As the Lord was passing by,
a fierce wind tore mountains and
shattered rocks ahead of the Lord.
But the Lord was not in the wind.
After the wind came an earthquake.
But the Lord wasn't in the earthquake.
After the earthquake there was a fire.
But the Lord wasn't in the fire.
And after the fire there was
a quiet, whispering voice.
When Elijah heard it,
he wrapped his face in his coat,
went out, and stood at the entrance of the cave.
Then the voice said to him,
"What are you doing here, Elijah?"
1 Kings 19:11-13 GOD'S WORD Translation
(You can insert your name in place of Elijah.)

CHAPTER EIGHTEEN

FINDING

A CHRISTMAS BRACELET

&

THE IRS

The ladies at my salon are among the most generous people I've ever met in my life. They're generous all year round, but their kindness gets kicked up a notch at Christmastime. They're also keenly aware that Christmas is my favorite time of the year. When most folks are hanging up their Halloween decorations, I've already started playing Christmas carols. Giving presents and receiving presents helps to spread the holiday cheer that we should experience all year round. In 1989, the ladies in my salon gave me a gift that still ranks up there with one of the greatest gifts I've ever received.

When I unwrapped the present and opened the small box, my eyes swelled up. I could feel the heat rising behind my eyes as my nose got stuffy and tears started rolling down my face. Stretched across my fingers, I held a beautifully made Plan of Salvation Bracelet. A delicately crafted cross dangled amidst the different colored collection of beads. All of the colored beads have a unique meaning and together they tell the story about why Jesus died on the Cross. I love to tell that story!

Let me tell you about what happened after I received that wonderful gift and then I'll tell you the story behind the Plan of Salvation Bracelet. God has a way of growing our generosity and he uses our kindness as a seed in his garden of goodness. I loved that bracelet so much that I wanted to give them as gifts to other people in my life. I first thought of my sister Karen, but there was one small problem; her wrists were too big for the bracelet. I didn't know how, but I wanted to finder a larger size. I prayed and asked God to please help me find a Plan of Salvation Bracelet for my sister Karen.

Later that week I had to run some errands after work. I needed supplies for the salon and I also need to fill out government paperwork for the salon at the IRS. Not having an exact time to be at either one, it was my choice regarding the order of my visits. While thinking about it, I felt that familiar "nudge" in my spirit telling me to visit the IRS Office first.

The first thing you do at the IRS Office is to perfect the fine art of waiting in line. That's an expected and begrudgingly accepted code of conduct. While standing in line, I noticed the lady standing in front of me was wearing the same kind of Salvation Bracelet that I had on. "Wow!" I said. "That's a beautiful bracelet and I have one just like it!" I lifted my arm, bent my wrist like a princess, and proudly displayed my bracelet. It was one of those electric moments when you've just realized that something extra special is happening. Your whole body becomes charged with an air of excitement and expectation. We instantly bonded and she quickly became my new sister in Christ.

In the next moment, the charge of excitement was elevated to another level. This lady just so happened to be in the business of making these beautiful wristbands and she would be happy to custom design larger sizes. After telling her about my prayer to have one made for my sister Karen, she responded with, "No problem!" God had answered another prayer and he did it in an IRS Office!

This very kind lady made one for my sister Karen, but she didn't stop there. I asked her to make one for the Pastor of the church I was attending along with a necklace for his wife. She had not previously made necklaces, but she gladly made one for me. It was another great Christmas of receiving, giving and praying!

The Plan of Salvation Bracelet is a great gift in many ways. I often just sit and use it in my prayer times. Sometimes in a traffic jam while traffic is at a dead stop, I look at my wrist on the steering wheel and think about the Way, The Truth and the Life as it's reflected through that bracelet. I'll hold one of the beads and reflect on its meaning and do the same for all of the beads. In the next few paragraphs, I'll describe the colors and what they represent.

THE PLAN OF SALVATION WRISTBAND

Black beads represent the sin that we all have. Sin separates us from God's Love. The Bible says that *"we've all sinned and fallen short of the glory of God." Romans 3:23 (NIV)* It also says *"For the wages of sin is death; but the gift of God is eternal life through Jesus Christ our LORD." Romans 6:23 (NIV)*

Red beads represent the Blood of Jesus Christ. His blood was spilled out on the cross as a sacrifice for the forgiveness of our sins. *"But God demonstrates his own love for us in this: While we were still sinners, Christ died for us." Romans 5:8 (NIV)*

White beads represent the purity of innocence. When we say we believe Jesus, it means we are professing our faith in him and that his death and resurrection have washed away our sins. *"But you know that he appeared so that he might take away our sins. And in him is no sin." 1 John 3:5 (NIV)*

Blue beads represent baptism which is a way of being immersed into the death and resurrection of Christ into new life. Our lives are now changed and baptism is an outward sign of what has happened to us spiritually. *"Those who accepted his message were baptized, and about three thousand were added to their number that day." Acts 2:41 (NIV)*

Green beads represent our growth as believers in Christ. True life change includes being teachable and the desire of pursuing the love of God in greater measures. *"But grow in grace, and in the knowledge of our Lord and Saviour Jesus Christ. To him be glory both now and forever. Amen." 2 Peter 3:18 (KJV)*

Yellow beads represent heaven and gold *"and the street of the city was pure gold." Revelation 21:21 (KJV)* As believers in Christ, we look forward to the day when he will take us to heaven to be with him forever. Jesus says in *John 14:2-3 (KJV), "In my Father's house are many mansions: if it were not so, I would have told you. I go to prepare a place for you. And if I go and prepare a place for you, I will come again, and receive you unto myself; that where I am, there ye may be also."*

Through the Cross, God gives us a pardon from sin that we don't deserve and we can't earn. Jesus did not wait until we stopped breaking God's commandments, He died for us while we still enslaved to sin. The Cross of Christ is a bridge of Love that allows us to cross over the separation between us and God. Without the Cross, we would fall into hell forever.

The Cross is our stairway to heaven as we walk in newness of life.

Jesus willingly died on the cross for you and me.

The Bible says that your life is changed

after you've been to the Cross:

"If anyone

is in Christ,

he is a new creation;

old things

have passed away;

behold,

all things have become new."

2 Corinthians 5:17 (NKJV)

CHAPTER NINETEEN

AN AUTUMN FALL ON A BIKE

Early one beautiful autumn afternoon I decided to go for a bike ride. The weather was perfect and I wanted to make the most of it so I made my plans quickly. Getting outside and hopping on my bike as fast as I could was my priority. Just before I closed the door behind me, I felt a "nudge" to go back and grab my jacket. Being in a hurry and not wanting to stop, I ignored the still small voice of advice.

Feeling the breeze blowing against my face as I cruised along on my bike gave me a great sense of freedom. While it was true that I had to be careful on the roads with traffic, the bike lanes did create a sense of security. After about an hour and a half, it was time to start heading home. So far it had been a pretty good ride, but that was about to change.

Traffic started to get a bit heavier as the late afternoon rush hour approached. As I began getting closer to where I lived, I felt that old familiar "nudge" again. That still small voice of advice was suggesting that I "get off the bike and walk with it." Once again I ignore the advice. "I was just around the corner from my home, so why would I stop and walk now? I asked myself. Leaning forward on the bike, I kept pedaling.

The traffic light ahead of me had just turned yellow, so I pedaled faster to get through the intersection before the light turned red. At that point, the speed I was travelling was probably a little too fast. There were railroad tracks crossing over the bike lane ahead of me. All of a sudden, I spotted a large amount of broken glass on the pavement. Wanting to avoid a potential flat tire (that would mean I would have to walk my bike) I swerved quickly to avoid the glass. That was a very bad move. Turning the handlebars quickly caused my rear tire to get caught in the railroad tracks and down I went.

Actually I didn't go straight down to the ground, my body was flung off the bike sideways and I was catapulted across the railroad tracks. I was sensible enough to have worn a bike helmet which protected me from a head injury, but my left elbow was not as fortunate as my head. My elbow was ripped by both the impact and the shattered glass. Moaning, I lay there for a few minutes before I was able to get up.

I was shaken badly and in a small way, I was glad no one stopped to see if I was okay and offer help. A lot of things were wounded, my body, my pride, my ego and my spirit. After I had checked the rest of my body and controlled the bleeding from my elbow, I picked up my bike. Forget about trying to ride it, even if the rim wasn't bent, I was too shaken to ride. Like a wounded duck, I walked my bike home.

It didn't take long for the embarrassment that I felt to be overridden by feelings of remorse. Sometimes God will give us guilty feelings in our guts over missed opportunities. I call these "convictions." I was convicted of not listening to the still small voice of advice. Not once, but twice I had ignore God's guidance. He had made recommendations which I foolishly ignored and now I was paying the price.

In the world there are moments of perfection, like a pitcher throwing a perfect game in baseball or a bowler rolling a perfect score of 300. Our communication with God is not going to be perfect, but he doesn't expect that from us. He also doesn't make communication with us complicated. He provides instructions in a simple, still small voice. The more we know someone, the better we understand how they communicate. My relationship with God was strong enough that I should have known better and listened to his advice. I felt remorseful, embarrassed and wounded. The only solution in moments like these is raw honesty and repentance. Admit you blew it and change your ways.

If I had listened to the first piece of advice about getting my jacket, it may have prevented some of the damage to my elbow. I ended up having to drive myself to Urgent Care where they pulled glass from my elbow and gave me 14 stitches. The doctor joked that I wouldn't be doing any elbow modeling anytime soon. I tried to force a smile at his lame humor, but that was like trying to squeeze a laugh out of a lemon.

It was a teachable moment and I shared it with anyone who asked about my bandaged elbow. Paying attention to God's warnings is extremely important. God isn't in the business of purposely causing us pain and suffering. He would rather see us experiencing joy in him and he'll give us a heads-up to help us avoid any unnecessary pain. The Bible says we will have trouble, but many times we can avoid trouble. Listening to God and doing what God tells us will help us avoid a whole heap of trouble in this world.

"I have told you these things,
so that in me you may have peace.
In this world you will have trouble.
But take heart!
I have overcome the world."
John 16:33

CHAPTER TWENTY

FAITH AND A RE-INFLATED LUNG

My brother-in-law Elmer was in the hospital facing surgery to remove one of his lungs. He'd been a heavy smoker most of his adult life and was previously diagnosed with tuberculosis. The doctors described his lungs as being comparable to that of a ninety year old man. Elmer was in very bad shape.

Only immediate family members were allowed into Elmer's room. The hospital's care team was afraid that germs could be potentially fatal due to his already frail condition. We were allowed in, if we wore masks and didn't bring anything in with us. In most cases, the patient is instructed to remove all jewelry or personal items from their body. Elmer wore a wristband with the letters, "WWJD." They were an abbreviation for "What Would Jesus Do?"

He was still a relatively young man in his fifties with a lot to live for. Elmer liked to work and was always busy doing something for his family. He loved his wife and children abundantly and, as a man of God, he remained teachable. Elmer was now praying for his life. If they took out one of his lungs, his ability to support his family would be greatly diminished. He poured his heart out to God and asked to be healed. His intentions weren't from a selfish heart; Elmer truly wanted to give his family the best life possible.

On the day before the surgery, while I was visiting Elmer with a mask on my face, the Lord spoke to me. He said to go get a Bible and read Psalm 91. I went down the hall to the visitor's waiting room where I found a Bible. With the Bible in my hands, I began to silently read the 91st Psalm. The Holy Spirit stopped me and told me to go back to Elmer's hospital room and read it out loud. This is what I read out loud in Elmer's room:

Psalm 91 New King James Version

Safety of Abiding in the Presence of God

91 He who dwells in the secret place of the Most High
Shall abide under the shadow of the Almighty.
2 I will say of the Lord, "He is my refuge and my fortress;
My God, in Him I will trust."

3 Surely He shall deliver you from the snare of the fowler
And from the perilous pestilence.
4 He shall cover you with His feathers,
And under His wings you shall take refuge;
His truth shall be your shield and buckler.
5 You shall not be afraid of the terror by night,
Nor of the arrow that flies by day,
6 Nor of the pestilence that walks in darkness,
Nor of the destruction that lays waste at noonday.

7 A thousand may fall at your side,
And ten thousand at your right hand;
But it shall not come near you.
8 Only with your eyes shall you look,
And see the reward of the wicked.

9 Because you have made the Lord, who is my refuge,
Even the Most High, your dwelling place,
10 No evil shall befall you,
Nor shall any plague come near your dwelling;

11 For He shall give His angels charge over you,
To keep you in all your ways.
12 In their hands they shall bear you up,
Lest you dash your foot against a stone.
13 You shall tread upon the lion and the cobra,
The young lion and the serpent you shall trample underfoot.
14 "Because he has set his love upon Me, therefore I will deliver him;
I will set him on high, because he has known My name.
15 He shall call upon Me, and I will answer him;
I will be with him in trouble;
I will deliver him and honor him.
16 With long life I will satisfy him,
And show him My salvation."

When I got to the last two verses, fifteen and sixteen, I felt God's overwhelming peace begin to grow inside of me. The confidence that God was going to do something powerful welled up inside me until it became a surging certainty. I knew, that I knew, that I knew; God was going to move on Elmer's behalf. I excitedly told Elmer and my sister Karen what had just happened. They wanted desperately to believe and I urged them to hang onto that belief. After that I left the hospital and went home.

The Bible is a beautiful book and often described as the Living Word because it comes alive for those who believe in it. The words written on the pages are "logos" which means "word" in the Greek language. The word comes alive as "rhema" when the Holy Spirit uses it for the purposes of God to answer prayer or give a message of instruction. Another way of explaining it, would be that logos is God's written word and rhema is when logos becomes his spoken word into our spirits. Logos with a capital "L" refers to Jesus as being the "Word." In John 1:1 (NIV) it is written; "*In the beginning was the Word, and the Word was with God, and the Word was God. "*

Elmer's surgery was scheduled for that very afternoon and I went home. Continuing to pray, the hours passed slowly until my sister Karen called. Her voice could only be described as a mixture between shock and joy as she relayed the events of the afternoon in the hospital. For some unknown reason, the doctors had delayed the start of his surgery and scheduled it for later that afternoon. As the time for that surgery approached, the doctors delayed it again and asked for another x-ray to be done. After viewing the x-ray, they found that Elmer's damaged lung had re-inflated itself! The doctors were baffled, but nonetheless, they cancelled the surgery altogether.

Doctors may be baffled, but God never is. There are times when we pray for healing that we almost try and manufacture faith. We try and force our minds to believe that God will move. The Holy Spirit will feed a real and genuine faith that will flood you with peace. God had released me from all doubt that he was going to do something for Elmer. God did not tell me what he was going to do and I don't have to know. I just have to keep on praying, believing and receiving, knowing that his Logos will become a living revelation of his Rhema. That's my way of saying; Jesus will give his Spirit to guide us in times of need.

"And I will ask the Father, and He will give you another Helper (Comforter, Advocate, Intercessor—Counselor, Strengthener, Standby), to be with you forever— the Spirit of Truth, whom the world cannot receive [and take to its heart] because it does not see Him or know Him, but you know Him because He (the Holy Spirit) remains with you continually and will be in you." John 14:16-17 (AMP)

CHAPTER TWENTY-ONE

THE HAIR-FISH AFFIRMATION

A lot of people have given advice through their own quotes of wisdom that begin with the words, "change is inevitable." The salon business could be called the "epitome of inevitable change." Something in hair salons is always changing, hair colors, hair styles, shampoos, clients, hair stylists etc. Our salon had gone through a major change and the biggest change took me by surprise. The level of respect among the hair stylists changed in a negative way.

My partner had won the lottery and no longer desired (or had a need) to be in the salon business. I agreed to buy her out and become the sole owner of the business. At the same time the model of doing business shifted from an "employee-based" salon to an "independent contractor" style where hair stylists would rent their own stations. New people came in and the levels of respect seem to be exchanged for competitiveness. The family atmosphere we had worked so hard to create was not what most hair stylists wanted. They were here to make money, no matter the cost.

Please don't misunderstand me; we still had some super nice people working there. The problems stemmed from the high turnover among hair stylists which is the norm in our business. I told God about my feelings and I poured out my heart to him. I like building relationships with people and I was frustrated by the lack of respect. If everyone helped each other, we'd all be a lot better off. My prayers to God weren't about asking him to change anybody or anything; I just needed to get this burden off my chest.

One of the things that I enjoy the most in my life is getting together with like-minded women at a teaching conference. I took some time off from work to attend a great conference about an hour and a half from my home. I met some new friends while I was there including a wonderful woman named Susan who's still one of my best friends today. Susan called me while I was driving home from the conference and on my way to work. She asked if I could schedule her for a hair appointment later that day. I had a full schedule due to the fact that I had taken time off, but I agreed to fit her in at the end of my day, around 4 PM.

Even on the way home from the conference, and back at work in the salon, I continued to express my feelings to God. I wanted to be a Christian woman who respected my clients and fellow hairstylists. Some of them didn't have a relationship with God and had no idea how much he loved them. Doing business God's way means that you try to set an example of putting others before yourself. I found that enjoyable, as a leader I wanted to teach that.

Susan arrived for her appointment and we had a great conversation. It was a delight to have my new friend as my newest client. This was the beginning of what has turned into a life-long friendship with God as our common best-friend. Susan left and it was time to clean up after an extremely busy day. Susan's hair was still on the floor as I began to sweep. Moving the broom quickly, I just wanted to get done and go home. I was very tired and my energy was almost gone. As I started to sweep away the hair from underneath my salon chair, my eyes suddenly were pulled to a small clump of hair in the shape of a fish. The hair seemed to cling to the slanted base of my salon chair. I leaned the broom against the counter and bent down for a closer look. It looked exactly like the shape of a Christian fish!

I stood up to get some scotch tape so I could tape the fish right to the chair where I found it. I wanted others to see it! I got down on my knees and taped the hair-fish to the chair. At that moment, bending over in my salon and on my knees taping a Christian "hair-fish" to a salon chair, the Holy Spirit quietly spoke to me in a still small voice; **"This is my affirmation that you belong to me. You are mine."**

Peace, tears, smiles, joy, and amazement – all of these wonderful feelings welled up inside me as I experienced God's personal touch. I was having sad feelings about the disrespect among people in the salon. I hadn't asked God for anything, I just spoke vulnerably and honestly. He answered with an affirmation. Sometimes our relationship with God is just about having a still small conversation from our hearts.

The History of The Christian Fish

There are a few different stories about the Christian Fish and how it came to be, but I will tell you what I've heard. In the days of Roman persecution, Christians developed secret ways of communication.

The fish was used above doorways, in the streets and on the ground. Some folks would draw a curved line on the ground and if someone else connected that curved line with another one it would form the shape of a fish. They would both know they were Christians at this point.

One other fact that I heard about was the ancient Greek word for fish which is, "ichthys." The letters form an acronym for the words that mean "Jesus Christ God's Son Is Savior."

The Christian Fish is known today throughout the world as one of the symbols of Christianity.

"If you've gotten anything at all
out of following Christ,
if his love has made
any difference in your life,
if being in a community of the Spirit
means anything to you,
if you have a heart, if you care—
then do me a favor:
Agree with each other,
love each other,
be deep-spirited friends.
Don't push your way to the front;
don't sweet-talk your way to the top.
Put yourself aside,
and help others get ahead.
Don't be obsessed
with getting your own advantage.
Forget yourselves long enough
to lend a helping hand."

Philippians 2:1-4 The Message

CHAPTER TWENTY-TWO

GOOD PLANS INTERRUPTED

Human nature in a person known as a Christian will generally compel them to do good works. This means that we perform actions of love toward other people. It feels good to help other people, but helping other people does not mean you have a relationship with God. Sometimes we make plans in our hearts without taking into consideration the bigger plan in God's heart. He will change our well-intentioned plans in order to teach us about our most important assignment in life, a personal relationship with Christ.

My plans to meet with a young lady after work were continually being interrupted. I was excited about the opportunity to mentor and disciple a woman whom I had met at the salon. A lot of small things were stealing my time as I tried to finish serving all my clients and be on time for our appointment. When I finally was able to get off the phone and end a long winded conversation, I went to the parking lot and found a flat tire on my brand new Honda Civic. I felt like a hopeless hurdler trying to overcome endless obstacles!

Walking back into the salon after discovering my flat tire, I called AAA Road Service. It would be awhile before they could send a service truck to repair my tire. There was no way I would be able to keep my appointment to mentor the young lady. My plans were shot and I was bummed. In the midst of my moment of self pity, one of the girls who worked in the Salon approached me. She asked if we could go to the facial room and speak to me privately. The facial room was a small area in the back of the salon and was currently empty.

As we sat down and she began to talk, I felt the Lord give me a Scripture verse from John 1:12-13 "But as many as received Him, to them He gave the right to become children of God, to those who believe in His name: who were born, not of blood, nor of the will of the flesh, nor of the will of man, but of God." (NKJV) The Lord further revealed to me that she was not born again. I asked her if she had a personal relationship with Christ. She said "Yes, I do believe in Jesus Christ." Then I asked her if she had a personal relationship with him. She then told me that she didn't know that she was supposed to have a personal relationship with Jesus.

Our conversation continued as I told her about two examples in the Bible of people who did good things, but weren't aware of the need to have a personal relationship with Jesus. Nicodemus and Lydia were both written about in the Bible and described as people whom the Lord opened their hearts. I asked her if she was "born again" and she wasn't sure what that meant. We then read from John 2:3 in the Amplified Bible, *"Jesus answered him, "I assure you and most solemnly say to you, unless a person is born again [reborn from above—spiritually transformed, renewed, sanctified], he cannot [ever] see and experience the kingdom of God."*

After that we prayed and she expressed her desire to make Jesus the Lord of her life and surrendered all to him. I asked if she had a Bible and she responded that she did not. I told her I would get her a Bible and that made her smile. I was at peace even though my original plans had been interrupted. God had taken my tunnel vision plans and enlarged them into his eternal plans.

I know what it's like to be a church-going religious person who thinks they're living a Christ-like life. It's easy to become entrapped in acts of neighborly service and forget about the more important personal relationship with God. Many people are drawn to churches by their moral code of conduct. Religion with a set of rules without a personal relationship with God is like trying to drive a car on an empty tank. I've learned that I need to include God in my plans or he won't hesitate to interrupt them. When God does interrupt my plans, I must surrender my plans to him and refocus my energies on his plan. Forcing our plans through repeated opposition isn't a good plan.

Speaking of cars, when the AAA Service guy finally showed up to fix my flat tire, he couldn't find anything that caused the flat tire. I guess it was just missing air! God will take the air out of our plans when we plan without him.

"One of those listening was a woman
from the city of Thyatira named Lydia,
a dealer in purple cloth.
She was a worshiper of God.
The Lord opened her heart to respond
to Paul's message."
Acts 16:14 (NIV)

"Go ahead and make all the plans you want,
but it's the Lord who will ultimately direct your steps.
We are all in love with our own opinions,
convinced they're correct.
But the Lord is in the midst of us,
testing and probing our every motive.
Before you do anything,
put your trust totally in God and not in yourself.
Then every plan you make will succeed."
Proverbs 16:1-3 The Passion Translation

"A man's mind plans his way [as he journeys through life],
But the Lord directs his steps and establishes them."
Proverbs 16:9 (AMP)

CHAPTER TWENTY-THREE

PAY ATTENTION TO DETAILS

The largeness of God's creation is astoundingly jam-packed with tiny details that we often overlook. There is nothing in God's vision that isn't worthy of our eyes giving it our full attention. We often miss moments of peace by not paying attention to small signposts pointing the way to God's love.

Being outdoors in nature helps me develop a deeper and more intimate relationship with God. Walking in the vastness of his mountain landscape draws me closer to him. It's almost like I can take a deep breath and inhale the immenseness of his creation surrounding me. Soaring birds, warm air, clouds, flowers, trees and the stillness of rocks make up the cornerstone of God's creation. As I hike though the mountain trails, my body and soul become a moving temple of fellowship in the Holy Spirit.

Even before I leave my home and head for the mountains, my excitement begins to build. I walk the 1.2 miles to the trailhead anticipating and expecting to spend time with God. I try and pay attention to details along the way, but I miss a few from time to time. I stopped in front of a church and looked at the beautiful flowers in the garden. I said to God, "It would be nice if those flowers were planted in the shape of a cross!" After a few moments of enjoying their scent and admiring their colors, I continued on to the mountains which were calling my name!

Being alone with God in nature creates an excellent classroom where he trains us in the finer points of his love. It's a time to listen, to observe, watch and pay attention to details. In a sense, the mountains are like God's throne and we are to approach his throne with confidence knowing he will provide us with grace and mercy in times of need. There in the moments of peace and tranquility, we receive strength for the times of trouble that are sure to come our way.

"Therefore let us [with privilege] approach the throne of grace [that is, the throne of God's gracious favor] with confidence and without fear, so that we may receive mercy [for our failures] and find [His amazing] grace to help in time of need [an appropriate blessing, coming just at the right moment]." Hebrews 4:16 Amplified Bible

After a few hours in the mountains I headed home. The Holy Spirit gave me a "nudge" to go back the same way by the church. As I passed the church, I once again slowed down to admire the flowers. I remembered that I had told God that it would be cool if someone had planted the flowers in the shape of a cross. Gazing at the flowers, I was astonished to see that some of them had been planted to grow in the shape of a Christian Fish! How had I missed that, it was beautiful!

Every day we miss small details in life, but thankfully we serve a God of second chances and comebacks. It's a good habit to develop a wider vision in expectation of becoming aware of God revealing his depth to us. Here are my "Seven A's For Attention To Details" – "Approach All things with An Attitude of Awareness And Anticipation." For those who are willing to see and hear, all of creation is God's classroom. As the final leaves fall from the trees in autumn, among Jesus final words on the cross that was made from a tree were these,

"Father, forgive them; for they know not what they do."
Luke 23:34 (KJV)

They took his body down from the wooden cross as the leaves fall down from the trees. The colors at the foot of the cross were the same as the freshly fallen leaves. Blood, sweat and tears mixed with clay mimicked the colors of orange, red, brown and yellow on the leaves now fallen down. His body was put into a grave behind a stone. The roots and branches of trees experience a winter frozenness that makes them appear dead. Jesus resurrection is the spring of eternal life. He was born again as the trees do in the spring. Are you born again?

"But blessed
[spiritually aware,
and favored by God]
are
your eyes,
because they see;
and
your ears,
because they hear."

Matthew 13:16 Amplified Bible

CHAPTER TWENTY-FOUR

THE SON OF A CLIENT

Owning a salon gave me a decent income and God blessed our business in tremendous ways. Still, the money we made wasn't enough to go traveling around the world or live a lavish lifestyle. I was comfortable, lived on a budget and stayed out of debt. Through our hiking club, I had met an older gentleman who helped me visit some places in the world I never would have been able to on my own.

My friend Jim Taylor and I were getting ready to hike Mt. Kilimanjaro, the tallest free standing mountain in the world. We trained for our trek up that long tall mountain by practicing on peaks with high elevation like Mt. Humphries in Arizona which was 12,633' tall. Mt. Kilimanjaro at 19,341' towered over Humphreys by another 6,708'. We were in decent shape, but we needed to get acclimated to the altitude that we would reach on Kili.

One other small problem I had was getting the right gear for a hike like that. Kilimanjaro is known as "Everyman's Everest" due to the fact that it is the easiest of the world's Seven Summits to climb as no technical climbing skills are needed. I left New York State many years ago and I don't like the cold when it gets in my bones! I needed to be warm, very warm. We would be hiking and sleeping in temperatures below freezing and I needed the proper clothing.

One of my clients at the salon came in one day for her regular appointment and said her son wanted to give me a jacket. This was no ordinary jacket; this was a North Face Heater Jacket. It had a heater built into the jacket. Her son wanted to give it to me, but there was one hitch, the heater didn't work. I was happy to have it and honored that my client's son wanted to bless me.

I took the jacket to REI, hoping that maybe they would know how to get it fixed. The man I spoke to advised me to write a letter (this was before we used email) to North Face and ask them if they could fix the jacket. So I went home and wrote North Face a letter and sent them the coat asking them to fix it. They sent me a reply that said they could not fix the jacket. Later on they sent another letter that said the jacket was worth $500 and would soon be sending me a check for that amount. I couldn't believe it; they sent me a check for $500!

Wanting to do the right thing, my conscience told me to call my client's son and tell him what happened. He told me to keep the $500! I knew God was blessing me big time through the generosity of my client and her son, but I was in for an even greater surprise. Within a few days, I had to file my income taxes. After doing my taxes, I found out that I owed the IRS $500. It would have been nice to have a heater jacket, but it was even nicer to have my taxes paid!

God always shows up on time, he created time. Surprises come in many forms and God likes to do surprises beyond our expectations and wildest dreams! Just for the record, and because you may be wondering, my friend Jim Taylor and I did make it to the top of Mt. Kilimanjaro. I was cold, but grateful that God had made a way. He gave me a generous friend who helped me go places I never would have gone on my own. He also gave me a client who had a generous son, willing to release a blessing to someone he didn't know.

When I reflect on the generosity of that mother's son, I think of how God was generous in giving us his son, Jesus Christ. Jesus made generosity into a way of life, demonstrating it through actions of love. He was always giving away love through acts of service. When we freely receive, it becomes natural to freely give. Giving is contagious.

"And I pray that you and all God's holy people
will have the power to understand the greatness of Christ's love.
I pray that you can understand how wide and how long
and how high and how deep that love is.
Christ's love is greater than any person can ever know.
But I pray that you will be able to know that love.
Then you can be filled with the fullness of God.
With God's power working in us,
God can do much,
much more than anything we can ask or think of."
Ephesians 3:18-20 International Children's Bible

"In the same way, the Son of Man did not come to be served.
He came to serve.
The Son of Man came to give his life to save many people."
Mark 10:45 International Children's Bible

"For God so [greatly] loved and dearly prized the world,
that He [even] gave His [One and] only begotten Son,
so that whoever believes and trusts in Him [as Savior]
shall not perish, but have eternal life."
John 3:16 Amplified Bible

CHAPTER TWENTY-FIVE

THREE EMMA'S AND MOTHER'S DOLL

The end of life is an unknown time period for most of us. Sometimes though, God gives us a "heads-up" when someone close to us is ready to leave this mortal world. My mother had lived a good life, but now it was time for her to embrace eternal life. We were being advised to move her from the hospital to a hospice care center. God had prepared me for this end of life event, but he also gave me an extra-special event in the midst of it.

Mom had been living in an extended care home where there were only about eight other residents. Her health had deteriorated to the point where they could no longer care for her and now she had been moved to the hospital. After a week in the hospital, the doctors said the best thing we could do is offer her the comfort of end of life care or hospice.

Facing the death of a parent is hard. I loved my mother and it was difficult to watch her life slide away. Joy was something that my mother always had, even as she slid deeper into the throes of dementia. She lost her ability to recognize people, but she never lost her ability to laugh with them. All of that joy faded just before she was moved to the hospital. It was as if someone turned a light off in my mother's soul and the laughter was gone.

Within two days of being moved to the hospital my mother became incoherent. She had been in a lot of pain and the nurses had put her on a special mattress to try and alleviate some of the pain. When the human body begins to shut down, all of its parts are affected. Knowing the end was near for my mother was sad, but it also brought a measure of peace. God had already prepared me for this season ahead.

On one rainy day, I was at home with a day off from the salon. I felt the Holy Spirit move me to begin putting all of my mother's affairs in order. That's what we do when we know that death is imminent. So I started organizing her personal papers and planning for her death. It's easier to accept the loss of someone you love when you know the inevitable is approaching soon. Readiness is an act that prepares the way for peaceful transitions.

On the day that we were moving my mother to the hospice care center, I gathered up all of her personal belongings from the hospital room. My mother didn't have many personal things left. Living in an extended care facility meant you didn't have a lot of room for personal stuff. Life has a way of downsizing our belongings as we grow older. Even our bodies begin to shrink! My mother did have something that was very precious and dear to her heart.

Ever since I was a little girl, and as far as I could remember, my mother had kept a small doll on top of her dresser. She never spoke about it or told us where it came from, but it was a fixture in my mother's life. It was now time to move my mother from the hospital to hospice. I grabbed several bags of her personal items including her doll and headed toward the hospital elevator. That doll was special to my mother and for that reason, that doll had become special to me.

The elevator door opened and I stepped inside joining a mother and her young daughter. The little girl was only about four or five years old. With her sparkling brown eyes and beautiful blonde hair, she lit up with a great big smile when she spotted my mother's doll. At that moment I felt the Holy Spirit nudge me to give the little girl my mother's doll. I asked her what her name was and she sweetly replied. "My name's Emma!" The tears immediately welled up behind my eyes and I could feel a burning in my heart. I leaned over and said to her. "This was my mother's doll and her name is Emma. Would you like to have my mother's doll?" That great big smile grew even bigger as I placed the doll in her arms and she hugged it tightly.

God gives us wonderful coincidences in life for many reasons. I think they're like signposts or cairns as we call them on hiking trails. They give us a hope for the future and confirm that we're doing the right thing. Listening to the still small voice of God takes practice and prayer. The rewards are peace and acceptance in times of grief and sadness.

This story would have ended here if it wasn't for what happened just a few moments ago. As I was writing this chapter about my mother named Emma and a little girl named Emma, my husband handed me a Drivers License. He found the license while serving at a community Thanksgiving Dinner at a church attended by hundreds of people. He asked if I would place the license in an envelope and place it in the mail. The name on the Driver's License was "Emma."

When an uncommon name appears in uncommon places, it's a good sign that the God who made the universe cares for each of us in a personal way. This has been a story about "Three Emma's." The story about the death and resurrection of Jesus includes an account called "On the Road to Emmaus." It may be a stretch for you, but it's just another God coincidence for me. Add a "U" to "Emma's and you have "Emmaus."

The story is about Jesus joining up with a couple of guys who didn't recognize him at first. Maybe you haven't recognized Jesus for who he is, but he recognizes you. Watch for signposts from God as he builds his personal story in your life. Trust me; your heart will burn inside you as everything becomes clear when you trust him.

Jesus Walks to Emmaus

"Later that Sunday, two of Jesus' disciples were walking from Jerusalem to Emmaus, a journey of about seventeen miles. They were in the midst of a discussion about all the events of the last few days when Jesus walked up and accompanied them in their journey. They were unaware that it was Jesus walking alongside them, for God prevented them from recognizing him.

Jesus said to them, "You seem to be in a deep discussion about something. What are you talking about, so sad and gloomy?"

They stopped, and the one named Cleopas answered, "Haven't you heard?

Are you the only one in Jerusalem unaware of the things that have happened over the last few days?"

Jesus asked, "What things?"

"The things about Jesus, the Man from Nazareth," they replied.

"He was a mighty prophet of God who performed miracles and wonders. His words were powerful and he had great favor with God and the people. But three days ago the high priest and the rulers of the people sentenced him to death and had him crucified.

We all hoped that he was the one who would redeem and rescue Israel. Early this morning, some of the women informed us of something amazing. They said they went to the tomb and found it empty. They claimed two angels appeared and told them that Jesus is now alive. Some of us went to see for ourselves and found the tomb exactly like the women said. But no one has seen him." Jesus said to them, "Why are you so thick-headed? Why do you find it so hard to believe every word the prophets have spoken? Wasn't it necessary for Christ, the Messiah, to experience all these sufferings and then afterward to enter into his glory?"

Then he carefully unveiled to them the revelation of himself throughout the Scripture. He started from the beginning and explained the writings of Moses and all the prophets, showing how they wrote of him and revealed the truth about himself.

As they approached the village, Jesus walked on ahead, telling them he was going on to a distant place. They urged him to remain there and pleaded, "Stay with us. It will be dark soon." So Jesus went with them into the village.

Joining them at the table for supper, he took bread and blessed it and broke it, then gave it to them. All at once their eyes were opened and they realized it was Jesus! Then suddenly, in a flash, Jesus vanished from before their eyes!

Stunned, they looked at each other and said, "Why didn't we recognize it was him? Didn't our hearts burn with the flames of holy passion while we walked beside him? He unveiled for us such profound revelation from the Scriptures!"

They left at once and hurried back to Jerusalem to tell the other disciples. When they found the Eleven and the other disciples all together, they overheard them saying, "It's really true! The Lord has risen from the dead. He even appeared to Peter!"

Then the two disciples told the others
what had happened to them on
the road to Emmaus
and how Jesus had unveiled himself
as he broke bread with them."
Luke 24:13-35 The Passion Translation

CHAPTER TWENTY-SIX

A VERY PRESENT HELP IN TROUBLE

Grieving the loss of a parent has a way of bringing the seasonal cycle of life and death into a very realistic perspective. On a very hot Arizona summer morning in late August at about 2:30 AM, I received a call from Hospice that my mother had just passed away. Even though I knew that call could happen at any moment, I wasn't ready. I don't have to describe to you what happened next as I began to tearfully grieve.

Calling my sisters and other family members would wait for a few hours. I thought it best to at least let them sleep through the night; there would be plenty of time to grieve. My sisters lived out of town and I was the only one who lived near the Hospice Center, so I became the family member designated to receive news about our mother's condition. Rolling over in a fetal position, I laid there for a few minutes knowing there was no way I could go back to sleep. I got up and drove to the Hospice Center, crying all the way there. I stayed with my mother and prayed for awhile until it got close enough to daybreak and I could head for the mountains.

There was no aimless meandering that morning on the mountain trails; I headed straight for my special place I called Prayer Rock. When I got there I sat down and cried, and I prayed. The Holy Spirit's presence was overwhelming. My body was moving back and forth as I rocked in grief. God's presence was with me in the rocking motions. It was like we were both gently swaying back and forth. He held me as we moved as one. He leaned with me to one side and then pulled me back to lean the other way. He was my very present help in my time of need.

Being the only family member who wasn't married meant that I would not have a spouse to console me. Sometimes though, even married people find themselves alone in times of grief. Some folks don't understand the grieving process and lack the knowledge or desire to show compassion and empathy. I had no one to lean on, But God. The Holy Spirit is our Helper and our Comforter when we desperately need him. Whether you have a spouse who supports you emotionally or not, leaning on God is where your heart will find its greatest comfort.

Around 6:30 AM, I began to make the family phone calls. With each call, I would relay the news about our mother's passing and then steady myself to listen to the loud wailing and agonized cries. The weeping lasted for a few minutes and then the funeral plans became the next topic of discussion. I was in Arizona, but my mother would be buried in Florida next to my father's grave. My sister Karen lived close enough where we both could meet in Phoenix and fly together to Florida.

If I had to pick a time for my mother to pass away, this was a pretty good time. It was around Labor Day weekend and I wouldn't have to take time off from work to travel from Arizona to Florida. It was easy to book a bereavement flight and everything went smoothly. The funeral service and burial would happen at the same church where my mother and father had attended when they both were alive. They had purchased burial plots in the church cemetery so we didn't have the burden of making last minute decisions.

As I prepared to give the Eulogy for my mother, I was flooded with peace. I knew I would see her again in heaven, in fact I would see both my mother and my father. It may have taken many years, but all of us had developed a personal relationship with Jesus Christ. We knew that through our belief in his death and resurrection, we would be given new life once our mortal bodies passed away. There's a great comfort in the peace of Christ that surpasses all understanding.

My eulogy focused on that belief that we would all see our mother again and the reasons why. One of my main goals outside of that was to let people know how much the Holy Spirit wanted to be there for us in our grief. The seasons of life change around us and our own mortality is evidenced everyday through the death of folks we love and even those we don't know. The knowledge of family reunions in heaven will bring joy and peace to God's people on earth.

"But the Helper (Comforter, Advocate, Intercessor—
Counselor, Strengthener, Standby),
the Holy Spirit, whom the Father will send in My name
[in My place, to represent Me and act on My behalf],
He will teach you all things. And He will help you remember
everything that I have told you.
Peace I leave with you; My[perfect] peace I give to you;
not as the world gives do I give to you.
Do not let your heart be troubled, nor let it be afraid.
[Let My perfect peace calm you in every circumstance
and give you courage and strength for every challenge.]
John 14:26-27 Amplified Bible

"God is our refuge and strength
[mighty and impenetrable],
A very present
and well-proved help
in trouble."
Psalm 46:1 Amplified Bible

CHAPTER TWENTY-SEVEN

COURAGE ISN'T TERMINAL

Sometimes we're given a season of rest between times of grieving. Sometimes grief seems to fall on us like autumn leaves; we keep experiencing grievous losses in quick succession. Grief becomes a season unto itself, but when we give our grief to God, the colors of ashes and dark bitterness can turn into the brightness of hope for a new day.

My sister Karen was about three years older than I was. She was my rock, my cheerleader, my role model, my closest friend and confidant. Karen struggled with cancer for seven years and died eight and a half years after my mother had gone to heaven. It was a long, hard battle, but throughout the whole ordeal, my sister was like the poster child for courage, bravery and joy in the face of adversity.

Karen used her battle with cancer to help other people. She faced the terminal assault on her life with a cheerfulness that betrayed the deadliness of the disease. As a pediatric nurse, Karen had a deep love for children. She took a special interest in any children who couldn't be loved by their own mothers. Her home was open to any child who needed love and a place to stay. Even teenagers, who had either run away from home or were kicked out of their homes, could find a home with my sister. In the midst of her painful battle, Karen was full of compassion and extended her heart to help others.

Like the leaves that lose their color in autumn, any glimmer of hope we had for healing began to fade. God would have to do a miracle to reverse this deadly disease and restore her badly decayed body. Not everyone in this world receives the healing that we pray for. There are many questions we have that won't be answered this side of heaven. God always gives the ultimate healing, this I know, for the Bible tells me so. That may sound like an overused cliché, but it's true. You can read what I know for yourself in Revelation 21:4 in The Passion Translation, *"He will wipe away every tear from their eyes and eliminate death entirely. No one will mourn or weep any longer. The pain of wounds will no longer exist, for the old order has ceased."*

We started to accept the inevitable that Karen would soon be leaving this world and be transformed as she went to a place without pain. Her cancer may be terminal, but her courage could never be terminal and would live on through all the people who were touched by her love. With the specter of her imminent death hanging over us like a dark cloud, we did our best to go on with life.

My friend Grace and I were hiking in the mountains when my brother-in-law Elmer called. He gave me the news that they were moving Karen back into the hospital. He didn't speak the words, but the unspoken message was that Karen was nearing the end of her battle. I hung up with Elmer and cried on the side of a mountain. The Holy Spirit strengthened me and told me to release my sister to him. This was a struggle for me because I had been pleading with God to heal my sister for many years. To release her now almost seemed like a defeat. Still, my surrender brought me peace knowing that God had a better plan than mine. I was thankful to have a friend like Grace who compassionately shared my pain and supported me in a dark hour.

The phone call came early in the morning and left me with the same feelings that I had after the call from Hospice about my mother's death. After a short time in the hospital, my sister had been moved to Hospice. On this particular morning at around 6:00 AM, Karen's ordeal was now officially over. My closest friend and sister who had the heart of a lion, was no longer in pain.

It was a Saturday and my schedule was booked solid with appointments. I really struggled to get through that day, doing my best to care for the needs of my clients. Because I was so busy, I couldn't escape to the mountains and go to my prayer rock. That's what I normally do when I'm faced with life's hard times. I go and pray and spend time in the presence of God. I knew his presence was here with me in the salon, but I still had to give a part of me to my clients, I couldn't surrender all of me to him.

The next morning found me exhausted after a night of broken and disturbed sleep. In that fitful moment of weariness, God gave me a song. In those early morning minutes, I felt like my grief was refreshed in another wave of sadness. In the stillness, the words from a song began to bubble up in my spirit. The warmth in my heart stretched into a smile on my face and brought a feeling of deep peace. These were the words I heard in my spirit, "More than the greatest love the world has ever known, this is the love I give to you." My mind replayed the entire song and its melody over and over. God loves us more than the world could ever know and it's more than forever! God reached me right where I was and strengthened me in his comfort. The song is called "More" and was written by Riz Ortolani and Nino Oliviero.

Karen's funeral was filled with people and stories about the lives she'd touched before and after her battle with cancer. One woman tearfully told her story about Karen taking care of her baby. She had been an alcoholic and was unable to be a fit mother. Karen told her about Christ and took care of her child. That's what Jesus would do. Her courageous disposition in the face of excruciating suffering had stirred the hearts of many children and grownups too.

Only God knows for sure, but it may be possible that he spared my sister the pain of watching her husband Elmer die from cancer four years later. They had known each other since they were 15 years old. They loved their children with the deepest love a parent could ever know. Karen was a mother to the motherless, a friend to the friendless and, she was like Christ to those who didn't know the Love of God. More than forever, I will remember the courage and love of Christ that my sister lavishly poured on everyone she met.

Karen knew that her pain and suffering had a greater purpose in a hurting world. She lived like Christ lived; his suffering was used to bring many to know the eternal Love of God. My sister is now born again in Christ as she embraces her new life and lives in union with him. The Christ in her also lives on in me and all the other people she touched through her sacrificial way of living life. Karen was a sweet person who allowed others to know the sweet aroma of her life as an offering to Christ.

"You are God's children whom he loves.
So try to be like God.
Live a life of love.
Love other people just as Christ loved us.
Christ gave himself for us—
he was a sweet-smelling offering
and sacrifice to God."

Ephesians 5:1-2 International Children's Bible

CHAPTER TWENTY-EIGHT

KNEELING UNDER A WING

My friendship with Jim Taylor was one of the greatest blessings that God ever gave me. Because of Jim's generosity and kindness, I was afforded many opportunities to travel to places I'd only dreamed about. Hiking on Mt. Kilimanjaro and going on an African Safari are among the highlights of my travels with Jim. Great times however, are not without moments of danger. Just as we were about to board a plane for the safari, I was almost crushed by the wing of an airplane.

Before we climbed the tallest free standing mountain in the world, Mt. Kilimanjaro, we were going on an African Safari in the Serengeti. We wouldn't be shooting any animals, at least not with guns. The trip to this National Park was strictly for sightseeing and shooting a lot of pictures. The name Serengeti is derived from the Maasai language and means "endless plains." It's a huge area of 12,000 square miles of protected game reserves and conservation areas. The governments of Tanzania and Kenya both work together to maintain the endless plains.

Along with another group of folks going on safaris, we were driven to a small airstrip in a very remote area. It was so remote and unremarkable; the only thing that gave any indication of this being an airstrip was the presence of an airplane! This was an all new experience for me and much different than airports with huge planes on long runways. The plane waiting for us was very small, with room for only eight passengers and our luggage was limited to 25 pounds or less. I had packed light with my camera taking up more room than anything else.

As the crew was loading the plane, I walked around and soaked in the beautiful remoteness of our surroundings. I couldn't go far because our departure time was approaching quickly. Still, my eyes travelled deep into the expanse of the wild nature around me. My mind marveled at how this land was so vastly different than my native Arizona. This scenery was spectacular! As I walked near the wing of the plane, my body was all of a sudden forced to the ground! I had no control as I buckled to my knees with my head forcefully tucked down into my chest. My heart felt like it was jammed up into my Adam's apple. My wrists and knees were numb with every other part of my body on pins and needles. I stayed in that kneeling or crouching position until I could finally relax and stand up. It was a moment or two before I found out what happened.

As they were loading the luggage onto the plane, the wing that wasn't anchored tilted suddenly and the whole plane leaned over sideways. The added weight on one side acted almost like a teeter totter when one person suddenly jumps off suddenly leaving the other to crash to the ground. If I hadn't been "pushed to my knees," I most likely would have been crushed by that wing. My friend Jim rushed over to me to see if I was alright as the other passengers crowded around me in disbelief. I was shaken, but there were no injuries to my body. After learning that I was okay, Jim's next question was "How did you know to get down when that wing came crashing over your head?" I smiled and said, "The only answer I can give you is, it must have been God!"

The only way I can describe that whole episode is that something welled up in my gut and wrenched my body down. I had no control whatsoever. I was not aware of the wing lurching over my head. All I know is that my body was reacting to a force within my body and I made no decisions at all in the whole event. Jim was astounded and I think it affected him deeply and strengthened him in the matter of his faith. God had come alive in a personal way with perfect timing. Anyone who witnessed this unlikely turn of events would most likely be strengthened in their faith as well.

I knew in my heart that God had pushed me down under that wing. There is no doubt in my mind. There are times in life that God spares us pain and tragedy before it can touch us. Some folks talk about cars swerving to avoid crashes or a gut feeling strongly urging them to leave a building or a relationship. Sometimes the Holy Spirit gives us foreknowledge to aid us in making wise decisions. Other times he just takes matters into his own "hands" and pulls or pushes us out of harm's way.

Remembering episodes like this help me to have greater faith and confidence as I face challenging or potentially dangerous situations. God can move faster than we can blink our eyes or he can wait until we've learned all we need to know in a situation. When we don't pay attention to what he's trying to tell us, we may end up in a ditch or he could let the wing of an airplane pummel us into the ground. We serve a God of suddenlies and he can bring anything into creation in an instant. He can also remove anything from creation in an instant. He alone knows how much time he's allotted for us to be here on earth. It's important to be ready, because someday, you'll suddenly meet him.

"It will only take a second. We will be changed as quickly as an eye blinks. This will happen when the last trumpet sounds. The trumpet will sound and those who have died will be raised to live forever. And we will all be changed."
1 Corinthians 15:52 International Children's Bible

CHAPTER TWENTY-NINE

AN APOLOGY FOR UNKIND THOUGHTS

We often think of our minds as private sanctuaries where we dwell alone with our solitary thoughts. What we think about in private is a reflection of who we will become in public. Our thoughts are the collective sum of our good character traits and our bad character traits. Our closeness with God can be measured by the distance between the two. As a fairly new Christian, I was just beginning to learn how God wanted to get rid of the "old me."

A regular client came into the salon to get his hair cut. He never had an appointment, but he always asked for me, and then waited until I was available. While I was in the middle of cutting his hair, I began having unkind thoughts about him. They were judgmental, disparaging and insensitive. I was thinking wrong thoughts. I did not know this man outside of the salon and didn't possess any intimate knowledge regarding his life or personal habits. My mind just wandered into a place of unkindness.

Finishing my day, I went home, did some chores, ate dinner and went to bed. At about 3 AM, the Holy Spirit woke me up in a way I can only describe as having an itch deep inside me that I couldn't scratch. Guilt was slowly spreading through my veins as I heard him say, "Your thoughts were unkind toward that man." I was shocked as the tears formed; my conscience grew overwhelmed with shame and remorse.

My pillow was wet with tears as the river of disgrace ran its course through my guilty conscience. Meekly, in a quivering whisper, I asked the Holy Spirit what I should do and he said,

"I want you to apologize." Imagine that, God wanted me to apologize to someone for my private thoughts that only he and I knew about. I surrendered completely and agreed that I would confess my unkind thoughts to the man and apologize. I would tell him I was sorry and would ask him to forgive me for my unkind thoughts.

By chance, or coincidence, or most likely as planned by God, I happened to see my client while exercising at the local gym. Like a coward, I avoided him and made my way out the door before he noticed me. I wasn't ready to apologize and that just deepened my guilt. How do you apologize to a client for thinking badly about them? As a new Christian, God was trying to teach me to work on my thought life. It's a wonderful thing to pray, go to church and study the Bible, but my thought life should line up with the truth of his Word. The Bible teaches us to renew our minds as God cuts away the flesh of our old selfish-life. As we mature in our relationship with Christ, he changes what we find as good and acceptable.

"And do not be conformed to this world [any longer with its superficial values and customs], but
be transformed and progressively changed [as you mature spiritually] by the renewing of your mind [focusing on godly values and ethical attitudes], so that you may prove [for yourselves] what the will of God is, that which is good and acceptable and perfect [in His plan and purpose for you]."
Romans 12:2 Amplified Bible

The following week after I had pulled my disappearing act in the gym that man walked into the salon for a haircut. As usual, he asked for me and waited as I finished another client's hair. I was getting misty eyed and nervous while I cut his hair. When I finished, I asked him if we could talk privately outside the salon. Sitting on a bench just outside the front doors, I was broken and started to cry.

I said to him, "I need to ask your forgiveness for having unkind thoughts about you." His response was to ask if he had done anything wrong. I assured him that this was all on me. God had shown me that my thoughts were wrong and I had no excuse so I had to apologize. He accepted my apology and forgave me. Our professional relationship became stronger as a trust was forged through honesty and transparency.

We have to work out our thought lives and God had me on a short leash. The closer you get to the Holy Spirit, the sharper his two-edged sword of Truth becomes as it cuts away the flesh of our old habits. He wants me to clean up my thought life. It would be a good idea for all of us to clean up our thought lives and renew our minds in God's Love.

"Finally, believers,
whatever is true, whatever is honorable
and worthy of respect,
whatever is right and confirmed by God's word,
whatever is pure and wholesome,
whatever is lovely and brings peace,
whatever is admirable and of good repute;
if there is any excellence, if there is anything worthy of praise,
think continually on these things
[center your mind on them,
and implant them in your heart]."
Philippians 4:8 Amplified Bible

"Who can live in your tent, Lord?
Who can dwell on your holy mountain?
The person who lives free of blame,
does what is right, and speaks the truth sincerely;"
Psalm 15:1-2 Common English Bible

CHAPTER THIRTY

FOREVER VISION IN THE GRAND CANYON

Each experience with God is similar to a fingerprint; each one is unique. The character of God never changes, but his mercies are new each day. "He's the same yesterday, today and forever." The Bible uses those words to describe Christ in Hebrews 13:8. He's always there, but in a different way on all of our days leading up to forever. When I'm hiking on a desert trail, in the forest or in the mountains, I can sense his presence in the beauty of his created nature that surrounds me. Sometimes though, God's presence seems to overwhelm all of my physical senses at once.

On a Fourth of July weekend, my friends Jim, Alyssa and I took a trip to go camping near Mt. Humphreys. At 12,633 feet, the mountain is the tallest in Arizona and the 12th highest in the US. The trailhead is about 11 miles north of Flagstaff. We were going to hike in and camp on the backside of Humphreys and make that our base camp for more hiking over the weekend. Just as we started setting up our tents, dark clouds began moving over the top of the peaks towering above us. Mountains are notorious for making their own weather, so you have to be prepared for storms, no matter what the weather report says.

It's kind of useless trying to continue putting up a tent in a rainstorm. It may have been the Fourth of July, but the temperature in the mountains can dip below 50 degrees. Add in a pretty ferocious wind and a constant downpour, the dampness had a way of influencing your desire to stay in a soggy sleeping bag inside a drenched tent. As puddles formed at our feet, we quickly gathered our wet gear and took off.

Jim asked if we had any ideas on where to go next. I suggested going to the Grand Canyon which was less than two hours away. The three of us agreed and we drove off toward the Canyon. It was a holiday weekend, but we were still able to get a reasonably priced motel room for the three of us to split the cost. Before drifting off to sleep, we discussed our options for the next day. Jim suggested hiking the Rim Trail which was flat and easy, but still afforded spectacular views of the Grand Canyon. Alyssa and I liked the idea and went to sleep in our dry beds.

We planned to hike about six miles and take a shuttle back to where we'd parked. Alyssa and I were hiking well ahead of Jim and enjoying ourselves immensely. We were singing worship songs as we walked along the edge of the Grand Canyon. It wasn't long before I felt God's overwhelming presence come over me. My body was overpowered to the point where I was moved to rest on a rock just a few feet from the edge of a cliff. From that rock, you could see – as far as the eye could see.

As I sat there, I heard the Holy Spirit say, "Think of a world without end." You can't see the other end of the Grand Canyon because it's so vast." Many times while I'm in nature, I can sense God's presence, but it's rare that he would also speak. I think it's because the combination of more than one of my physical senses being affected by his power is too much to bear. My thoughts began to imagine what it must be like living in heaven forever, in a place of seeing God's glory, forever and ever.

I was aware of people walking by on the trail, but I was laid out on the rock and weeping uncontrollably. After awhile I thought maybe it was time for me to get up and move on, but I didn't want to disturb the beauty of the moment that I was in with God. The Holy Spirit seemed to be acting like a friend who wasn't quite ready for our visit to be over. I remained where I was; it became my rock of refuge from the busyness around me. I stayed affixed to that rock until I knew he was releasing me.

Jim had finally caught up with us and asked me if I was okay. Alyssa was excitedly asking me what God had said because she knew what had happened to me. It was hard for me to launch into an explanation about what had just happened. Having a human conversation after having a heavenly conversation can be like trying to explain God to your cat! Your mind is still in a higher spiritual plane and trying to explain it is like purposely numbing your taste buds. I knew Alyssa understood and I believe Jim was gathering bits and pieces of information that would give him understanding.

All of us are different and unique just like every experience we have with God. Too often we judge people through the lens of our own experiences. We all gather information through separate and distinct characteristics as individuals. That helps us gain understanding as we organize information to give us greater insight into what we're trying to learn. Being separate in the way we understand things does not prevent us from all being loved as individuals by an all loving God who created us that way.

Sometimes I quietly bask in the beauty of God's creation. Sometimes I dwell expectantly in the beauty of a word that he's spoken over me. Sometimes I weep with gratitude in the beauty of an answered prayer. Sometimes I simply dwell in his presence and express my appreciation for loving me. Sometimes his presence is like a tsunami of grace, clearing the way for me to see his never ending glory in a vision of heaven over the Grand Canyon.

"Now to Him who is able
to [carry out His purpose and]
do superabundantly more
than all that we dare ask or think
[infinitely beyond
our greatest prayers, hopes, or dreams],
according to His power
that is at work within us,
to Him be the glory in the church
and in Christ Jesus
throughout all generations
forever and ever.
Amen"
Ephesians 3:20-21 Amplified Bible

"Jesus Christ is
[eternally changeless, always]
the same yesterday
and today and forever."
Hebrews 13:8 Amplified Bible

"But let them all be glad,
those who turn aside
to hide themselves in you.
May they keep shouting for joy forever!
Overshadow them in your presence
as they sing and rejoice.
Then every lover of your name
will burst forth with endless joy."
Psalm 5:11 The Passion Translation

CHAPTER THIRTY-ONE

BETRAYAL & FORGIVENESS

Some life-events can leave you with a troubled soul, a deep heartache and a very bad taste in your mouth. Betrayal comes in many forms and they all carry the potential of devastating effects leading to long term negative consequences. I was betrayed by someone who was both a friend and a client. For a season of my life, the release of emotional pain and getting past the resentment of betrayal became mountains I had to climb.

When my unfaithful friend asked for forgiveness, I knew I had to do what Jesus would do. Even as he was still in the midst of suffering betrayal and rejection at the hands of his torturers, he still focused on forgiveness. While he was nailed to the cross, Jesus said these words as recorded in the Bible:

"When they came to the place called The Skull,
there they crucified Him and the criminals,
one on the right and one on the left.
And Jesus was saying,
"Father, forgive them;
for they do not know what they are doing."
Luke 23:33-34 Amplified Bible

It's easy to slip on one of those silicone wristbands with the letters "WWJD", meaning "What Would Jesus Do." The fact of the matter is, none of us is capable of doing what Jesus did. Still, acknowledging that he is the Way, the Truth and the Life establishes a personal foundation for making decisions. Forgiveness is written about all over the Bible, but until we're faced with gut-wrenching betrayal, forgiveness is a great discussion topic.

My friend and client called me on the phone and said she was sorry. I told her she had my forgiveness. The words were easy, believing in them was nowhere near easy! Although the apology and forgiveness were spoken, there seemed to be some truth that was missing. She remained my client and friend, but we never spoke about it again. It seemed like there were words left unspoken which prevented real closure to the deception and dishonesty.

Early one Friday morning, my friend came into the salon for a hair coloring appointment. The process of hair coloring required a waiting period for the color to set. Sometimes that presented an opportunity for conversation. As we chatted, the Holy Spirit told me that my friend needed to forgive herself. When I repeated that message to her, she looked away and said, "I don't think I do."

Not really sure of what would happen next, I felt the Holy Spirit leading me to take my friend into the Facial Room. It was in the back of the salon and afforded the possibility of greater privacy. The Holy Spirit directed me to have my friend sit on the table and I was to sit on a stool. She was in a higher position than me, and that was the beginning of what God was trying to teach me.

Being in a position of humility, I was being instructed not to take a position of superiority. It's easy for someone who has been betrayed to take on the attitude and character of being a martyr. The knowledge that God wanted to impart into my heart began pouring in like a spring rain. He loved her as much as he loved me. He was no respecter of persons. He hurt for her as much as he hurt for me. She was suffering because of her betrayal and the Holy Spirit would not allow me to have an attitude of haughty superiority.

Our words were few, but by the end of our time, I believe she knew what the Holy Spirit wanted her to know. She had been stuck in a place of not believing she was really forgiven. I let her know that God looked at her with grace filled eyes of forgiveness. In my heart, I believe that she finally understood the unsurpassed compassion of God.

As I write this, the leaves are falling outside my window and rain is pouring down. It's an annual act of surrender for the trees in Buffalo, N.Y. as their branches give a complete acquittal to the foliage from a season about to end. After a season of rest, the trees spring into a new life.

God plants the nature of his character in the created world around us. Betrayal is painful, but unforgiveness without God's grace, results in the fall of man, never to see spring again. Forgive in Christ and live Life eternal.

"And become useful *and* helpful
and kind to one another,
tenderhearted
(compassionate, understanding, loving-hearted),
forgiving one another
[readily and freely],
as God in Christ forgave you."

Ephesians 4:32 Amplified Bible, Classic Edition

CHAPTER THIRTY-TWO

THE VALUE OF A PURSE

Looking back on my life, I can see many episodes that have shaped my character and personal habits. The roots of life experience can stretch deep and affect the decisions we make on a daily basis. I may not have grown up in extreme poverty, but my family did struggle to provide some of the basic necessities like housing and health care. I think one of the greatest forms of poverty is the lack of hope or believing in yourself.

My Dad complimented me on my perseverance and work habits after he had become a senior citizen. When life slows down as people age, they have more time to reflect and notice small things. Maybe Dad noticed my ability to be frugal and have a healthy respect for money. It's not hard for a kid growing up to notice the wealth of other families and grow resentful. That wasn't the case for me, but there were some other habits that affected the way I looked at money.

Having very little in the way of money and personal possessions can almost cause someone to construct their own personal caste system. As a child, I wore hand-me-down clothes and I couldn't wait until I had a job so I could buy my own clothes. Children can view themselves as unworthy of the things that wealthier people have. Deep inside their self-conscious grows a shameful attitude that disdains the very thought about having money. Unworthiness becomes a personal currency that takes up residence inside their purse. It becomes taboo to even think about buying things that cost more than average. It's a mindset of poverty with childhood roots.

After I had become a Christian, I would read Bible passages about God being a generous Father who wouldn't withhold anything from his children. In my heart lived a generous little girl who loved to give gifts to as many people as she could. That little girl wasn't alone; she lived with an older woman who couldn't understand that God wanted to give her the gift of receiving. It was hard for me to receive and it was hard for me to even desire a good and expensive gift. I wanted to believe that God desires to give us abundantly above and beyond whatever we could imagine.

Purses are valuable in many ways and sometimes they can even reveal a woman's personality. I had admired Brighton Purses for a long time. They were excellently made with quality materials, durable, long lasting, beautiful and expensive. In my heart of hearts, I desired to have a Brighton Purse, but didn't think I should spend that kind of money on myself. It was almost a feeling like I didn't deserve to have something so nice. In theory, window shopping is a safe pastime because it keeps a pane of glass between you and the item you'd buy if you could. I admit to being a Brighton Purse window shopper, but it was just a dream.

My good friend Susan came to church one Sunday with a beautiful Brighton Purse slung over her shoulder. Susan is an intelligent and classy lady who always presents herself with dignity and compassion. I admired her in so many ways. I remarked on how beautiful she looked. And then I said, "I like your new purse too!" I then joked with her that if she ever wanted to give that purse away, I'd be happy to receive it!

Three years later, Susan once again came to church on a Sunday morning. She was carrying a big box and smiled as she walked toward me. I was just leaving the first service and Susan was arriving for the second service. Susan handed me the box on the sidewalk just outside the front doors of the church. I opened the box and found the Brighton Purse that I had so admired three years earlier. I cried as I set it down and gave Susan one of those great big heart to heart hugs. Through my good friend Susan, God gave me a desire of my heart.

Only God knew my desire to have a Brighton Purse that was hidden in the confines of my heart. That desire was buried deep underneath many layers of believing that I was undeserving and unworthy. God unearthed that desire with his undying love. He is still teaching me about the value of receiving. He's still teaching me to value myself the way he values me. Paraphrasing what Jesus said when he was asked about the greatest commandments, he said, "Love God with your whole heart and love your neighbor the same way you love yourself." I had to get it through my head that if I loved God with my whole heart and I loved to give love to my neighbor, then I must be willing to receive that same love unto myself.

Poverty is the mindset of an empty heart. Our strengths of giving may cover up our weaknesses in receiving. There is much truth in the old adage that says, "You reap what you sow". Some folks struggle in letting their hearts become receiving grounds for the reaping to take place. A giving person who isolates themselves from receiving will not reap the abundant generosity of God.

God created us as compassionate reflections of his grace and mercy. It is true that it's better to give than receive, but receiving can enlarge your understanding of how much God gives ever more abundantly every day.

"For the Lord God is a Sun and Shield;
the Lord bestows [present] grace and favor
and [future] glory (honor, splendor, and heavenly bliss)!
**No good thing will He withhold from those who walk
uprightly."**
Psalm 84:11 Amplified Bible, Classic Edition

"Look at the birds of the air;
they neither sow [seed] nor reap [the harvest]
nor gather [the crops] into barns,
and yet your heavenly Father keeps feeding them.
Are you not worth much more than they?"
Matthew 6:26 Amplified Bible

"They may weep as they go out
carrying their seed to sow,
but they will return with joyful laughter
and shouting with gladness
as they bring back armloads of blessing
and a harvest overflowing!"
Psalm 126:6 The Passion Translation

CHAPTER THIRTY-THREE

A LADY WITH A SWORD

God has spoken to me in many ways in my life. Although I cannot give you a certain method that guarantees that you'll hear from God, I can suggest that it's best to remain teachable. Be open to understanding how God speaks in different ways. Here are the ways that God has made himself known to me;

1. **Through Prayer** ~ when we pray, it's more than just speaking to God; it's really more about listening. Praying before Thanksgiving Dinner can be a beautiful witness to family members, but praying in the Spirit opens up our hearts to receive what the Spirit has to say. *"With all prayer and petition pray [with specific requests] at all times [on every occasion and in every season] in the Spirit, and with this in view, stay alert with all perseverance and petition [interceding in prayer] for all God's people."* Ephesians 6:18 Amplified Bible

2. **Through His Word** ~ The Bible is a living word, meaning that it will apply timeless truths from eternity past to the present situations in our lives. It's best to be very familiar with what's in the Bible so you know what truth is and can identify words that distort the truth. God will use his Word in unity with a word from his Spirit and prayer. *"So stand firm and hold your ground, having tightened the wide band of truth (personal integrity, moral courage) around your waist and having put on the breastplate of righteousness (an upright heart), and having strapped*

on your feet the gospel of peace in preparation [to face the enemy with firm-footed stability and the readiness produced by the good news]. Above all, lift up the [protective] shield of faith with which you can extinguish all the flaming arrows of the evil one. And take the helmet of salvation, and the sword of the Spirit, which is the Word of God." Ephesians 6:14-17

3. **Through Other People** ~ God can use a friend, or a complete stranger to deliver a timely word to your heart. When someone does give you a word of knowledge or information, pray before you take any action. The world is full of false prophets and evil folks, whose purpose is to steal, kill and destroy God's love in you. The word of man must line up with the Word of God. *"He who pays attention to the word [of God] will find good, And blessed (happy, prosperous, to be admired) is he who trusts [confidently] in the Lord." Proverbs 16:20 Amplified Bible*

4. **The Circumstances In Our Lives** ~ God brings us down many roads to teach us lessons that will ultimately lead to enlarging his love in our hearts. Circumstances are like the pile of rocks or cairns that point the way up a mountain trail, they bring us to waypoints of decision and learning. *"So now I live with the confidence that there is nothing in the universe with the power to separate us from God's love. I'm convinced that his love will triumph over death, life's troubles, fallen angels, or dark rulers in the heavens. There is nothing in our present or future circumstances that can weaken his love." Romans 8:38 The Passion Translation*

5. **Through The Holy Spirit's Witness To Our Inner Spirit** ~ Jesus can give us a vision, the Holy Spirit can give us a Word and God can make us know the Father's Love. Some folks call it their conscience, intuition or gut feeling, but for those who develop a relationship with God, The Bible says we are "made in the image and likeness of God." (Genesis 1:27) It's God's nature to speak to us. Knowing God and having his presence inside us will open our hearts and minds to his nature. *"The sheep that are My own hear My voice and listen to Me; I know them, and they follow Me." John 10:27 Amplified Bible*

Over the years, I've found certain Bible verses touching me in deeper ways than others, although this list changes with the seasons! These are the verses that sustained me, nourished me and gave me encouragement when I needed it the most. I pray that as you read them. The God who loves you will touch you in a deeply personal way.

"For the Lord God is a sun and shield;
The Lord bestows grace and favor and honor;
No good thing will He withhold from those who walk uprightly."
Psalm 84:11 Amplified Bible

"Therefore the Lord waits [expectantly]
and longs to be gracious to you,
And therefore He waits on high to have compassion on you.
For the Lord is a God of justice;
Blessed (happy, fortunate) are all those who long for Him
[since He will never fail them]."
Isaiah 30:18 Amplified Bible

"I would have despaired had I not believed that
I would see the goodness of the Lord
In the land of the living.
Wait for and confidently expect the Lord;
Be strong and let your heart take courage;
Yes, wait for and confidently expect the Lord."
Psalm 27:13-14 Amplified Bible

"The Lord God is my strength
[my source of courage, my invincible army];
He has made my feet [steady and sure] like hinds' feet
And makes me walk [forward with spiritual confidence] on
my high places [of challenge and responsibility]."
Habakkuk 3:19 Amplified Bible

"Now to Him who is able
to keep you from stumbling or falling into sin,
and to present you unblemished
[blameless and faultless]
in the presence of His glory
with triumphant joy and unspeakable delight,"
Jude 24 Amplified Bible

"Let us seize and hold tightly
the confession of our hope without wavering,
for He who promised is
reliable and trustworthy and faithful
[to His word];"
Hebrews 10:23

CHAPTER THIRTY-FOUR

MY THANKSGIVING FOR YOU

Having friendship with people who know the depth of God's Love is like being surrounded by your own personal cloud of witnesses. Friends, who believe in God, will believe in you. They will pray for you to experience the best God has to offer. Many people will walk through our lives as we age and become more mature in our walk with God. In this Chapter on Thanksgiving, I'm making an attempt to give thanks in writing to some of those many people. I know them as personal friends who've been sent by God to enlarge my heart into a place of greater Love.

As I write this Chapter, my soul is fresh with the good memories of another Thanksgiving celebration with my husband's family. It's a beautiful thing to have an entire extended family accept you as one of their own and love you completely. Thanksgiving's at the Reger's, Christmas's at the Sikora's are great family traditions. My heart smiles as I think of all the family warmth during those times.

From here on out in this Chapter, you will find the names of my personal cloud of witnesses. Thank you all for being in my life and bringing me closer to God. Jesus loves you and so do I.

Dr. Pamala Denise Smith
Her tenderness of heart, humility, wisdom and love of Jesus has inspired me to grow in the Word and the knowledge of Jesus.

Elaine Strahm

For having a willing heart to always seek the Lord on my behalf.

Dr. Mike Maiden

Your display of true courage in the face of fierce adversity is deeply imprinted on my heart.

Pastor's Jim & Sharon Roam

You are solid rocks in a world of shifting sands.

Pastor's Monty & Kelli Sears

Your unbridled passion for the Truth of "Jesus Christ" compels me to greater heights of His Love.

Pastor's Ken & Deanna Dutton

You have God's character of integrity, candor, and diplomacy. Thank you for believing in me and the vision God has placed in the hearts of Bob and myself.

Sally Smale

Your Revelation Teaching on the Song of Solomon reached the core of my heart and opened the eyes of my understanding of how deeply Jesus loves me.

Susan Baldwin

You're always willing, extremely capable, and totally trustworthy. We've laughed, prayed and cried together. I love you Susan.

Susan Barrios

Mere words cannot express my appreciation and heartfelt thanks to you, my sweet friend. Your generosity and loving-kindness is a model of God's immeasurable Love.

Jane Taylor
You are generous, gentle, fun loving, talented, timely, creative and charming – all wrapped up in one lovely lady.

Mike & Susan Diehm
You both always had my back in so many ways. You are both treasures in my heart.

Miguel & Maria Caballero
We have walked together through every valley and mountaintop of life. I so dearly love you and your family.

Grace Brazier
You were always there when I needed someone with your heart open wide. I love your winsome ways and determination to be all Christ intends for you.

Jim Taylor
My life and heart would be so empty without your steadfast companionship for so many years.

Patti McLaren
I'm grateful to have you as a fellow soldier and prayer warrior for Christ.

Patty Berens & The Monday Monthly Prayer Gathering
It's an honor to gather with women on the frontlines of ministry. You are all caring, kind, and gentle – fellow servants of Jesus Christ. I'm grateful to you Patty, for allowing me to be a part of the inner circle.

Brenda Wilmont
A friend who really loves me just the way I am; warts and all!

Pamela Williams

You are classy, intelligent and eloquent, thank you for your influence in my life.

Margy Granville

Thank you for all the many times you have spoken into my life, helping me to be healthy in my soul.

Jackie Stroh

You are a model of commitment and loyalty. Thank you for all the many times you've kept me in the loop!

Cathy Schwab

The gift of your friendship is a real answer to prayer for both of us. You are a real Abigail for the Body of Christ.

Rick & Jane German

You both always provided a safe haven to laugh and be nourished by true friendship.

The Entire Kuebler Clan

To Joe, Anna, Steve, Michelle, Karen & Jerry, Janet & Marion and Mary Ellen, thank you for making me a part of the family. I love you dearly.

Without Walls Prayer Partners

To Yolanda, Kathy, Debra, Barbara, we continue to fight the good fight of faith for His glory!

My Greatest Thanksgiving is most of all given to the Way, the Truth and the Life - Jesus Christ, who saved me from myself!

"First,
I thank my God through Jesus Christ
for all of you,
because your faith
[your trust and confidence in
His power, wisdom, and goodness]
is being proclaimed in all the world."
Romans 1:8 Amplified Bible

"[*A Call to Prayer*]
First of all, then,
I urge that petitions (specific requests),
prayers, intercessions (prayers for others)
and **thanksgiving**s be offered on behalf of all people,"
1 Timothy 2:1 Amplified Bible

ABOUT THE AUTHOR

Linda Kuebler is a prayer warrior, woman of great faith and a bird lover who likes to climb mountains. As a business owner and hair stylist for over 40 years, Linda loved to work with her hands as she ministered to the hearts of her clients.

Currently, Linda is the Co-Director with her husband Bob of a nonprofit ministry called Youth With A Purpose. The mission of YWAP is to help inner-city young people and their families become Christ-centered mentors for the next generation.

As a young child, Linda was always a "nature girl' who followed her curiosity in exploring the world around her. Her relationship with God deepens with the changing of seasons that cover the valleys and mountains of life. Her rugged determination helped her climb mountains and makes her a natural for teaching other people how to struggle through adversity.

At YWAP, Linda finds creative ways to help young people understand how God's love can move mountains. Addiction, abuse, and fatherlessness are mountains that can be overcome by teaching young people the Way of Truth and Life in God's Love.

Linda prays for people all over the world by phone and email. She was on the Prayer Team at Without Walls Church for many years. Her heart is to know Jesus more each day and help others know how much God loves them. Linda's determined purpose is to know Him.

"By your steadfastness and
patient endurance
you shall win the true life of your souls."
Luke 21:19 Amplified Bible, Classic Edition

"With all prayer and petition pray
[with specific requests]
at all times
[on every occasion and in every season]
in the Spirit, and with this in view,
stay alert with all **perseverance** and petition
[interceding in prayer]
for all God's people."
Ephesians 6:18 Amplified Bible

All proceeds from this book are used to help further the mission of Youth With A Purpose Inc.

YWAP is an inner-city youth ministry based in Buffalo, NY. We believe that all children are gifted on both sides of the womb. We exist to identify, nurture, protect and empower young people to use their gifts to be the world changers whom God created them to be.

Young people who have a fractured relationship with their earthly father are more likely to have a fractured relationship with their heavenly Father. We use Biblical Leadership Lessons combined with physical activities to help young people and their families grow healthy relationships spiritually, physically and emotionally.

The inner-city is plagued by addiction, abuse, violence, gangs and poverty. Young people are looking to fill an empty hole in their hearts. God is the only answer.

In September 2019, YWAP is launching the Great Dads Network to help teach young men about the responsibilities and joys of fatherhood.

Our Mission Statement
"We help young people and their families become Christ-centered mentors for the next generation."

You may reach us at: 716-830-8240
ywapbuffalo@yahoo.com
Youth With A Purpose 157 Locust Street Buff, NY 14204
www.youthwithapurpose.org

Online Donations are Tax Deductible and can be made through PayPal at:
http://www.youthwithapurpose.org/support-ywap.html